Antichrist Associates and Cosmic Christianity

Antichrist Associates

and

Cosmic Christianity

by
John Barela

TODAY, THE BIBLE AND YOU
BROKEN ARROW, OKLAHOMA

TODAY, THE BIBLE AND YOU
P.O. Box 1722 Broken Arrow, OK 74013

Printed in the United States of America

Table of Contents

Foreword

by Constance E. Cumbey

When I first began to notice the artifacts of the New Age Movement, I could not help but see a vast profusion of symbols.

Their use of the rainbow intrigued me.

I noticed that every time I saw a secular bookstore with a rainbow on the window, I could walk inside and purchase all the strange research materials I required.

Other symbols came to my attention as well. The yin-yang decorated everything from grocery store façades to martial arts studios. Apparent triple sixes adorned organizational letterheads ranging from the World

Antichrist Associates

Future Society to the Federal Aeronautics Administration.

I was soon to learn that symbols were a primary mode of communication between the New Agers. They were used to "reinspire" and communicate its underlying occultism. I learned, for example, that there was a dictionary of 50,000 "sigils."

I learned from a book explaining Rosicrucian doctrine that symbols were used to heighten altered states of consciousness as well.

For example, somebody might be taught to meditate to progressively deeper states by pondering the various levels of the rainbow. When one thereafter saw a rainbow, it would give him a fresh and synthetic experience — not to mention the reinforcing of the previously induced mystical experience.

Symbols are a fascinating example of occult bias of the particular sculptor who wished to place a little of his own philosophy in the masonry.

Sometimes this would even happen without the knowledge of the one commissioning the art of the architecture. One interesting example of this is contained in the book *Michelle Remembers* when Michelle discovered a Satanic symbol in a Catholic church she visited with her psychiatrist.

Upon her discovery the parish priest took the offending item out for burning. All present were surprised when there was an apparent demonic manifestation arising from the burning flames.

John Barela has found occult symbols and symbols bearing close resemblances to occult symbols in some very unlikely places.

They give rise to a belief that occultists have attempted to penetrate Christian circles and plant their symbols there for a very long time. There is, of course, always the possibility of coincidence, or that the artist liked the shapes and didn't know why.

But then again, there is the possibility that there was intentionality in the placing of these symbols — either by the artisan or by the person(s) or organization(s) contracted for the work.

At times you may find Rev. Barela's conclusions fascinating. Other times, you may find them infuriating.

But at no time will you find them boring!

Antichrist Associates

His is a fascinating and colorful study of the incursion of occult symbols into the Christian world and into our everyday lives.

Constance E. Cumbey
June 25, 1986

An Evil Plot

Dare we use the word:
"Conspiracy"?

Is there a secret, insidious, destructive, Satanic **conspiracy** afoot?

An evil plot?

Are we dabbling in paranoia to suggest that Satan has eased his claws into the ...

CHURCH?

Into our spiritual lives?

Into seemingly Christian denominations, movements, traditions, rituals, and organizations?

Consider these scenes:

• In the Vatican, the Roman Catholic Pope grants an audience to American school children on a special journey to Rome.

He wears his special garb, including the historic, famous, papal tiara, also known as the triple crown.

• A charismatic pastor, caught up in the fervor of his Sunday service, asks his church members to raise their hands and repeat after him over and over a "prayer in tongues." Worshipers do so, *innocently* believing they are moving closer to the Spirit of God.

• The newest initiate is welcomed at the local Masonic Lodge. He mistakenly believes his membership in the organization will enhance his service for both God and his community.

In all of these scenes the *power of Satan* is being exerted and a **link** between Christians and the occult is strengthened.

Subtly.

Insidiously.

Why?

It should be clear —

To usher in:

The Rule of the Antichrist

The book of Revelation predicts the coming of a one-world political and religious system.

According to the Holy Scriptures, there will be a tremendous unity across the entire planet under the rule of the Antichrist.

Many Christians have wondered how this can occur because there are so many different opinions throughout the world.

There are many nations, many languages, many different religious groups.

Today, there are organizations and world religions which would **seem** diametrically opposed.

Be not deceived!

In reality these groups are working together under Satan to bring about a unified system.

Lucifer's deception, which began in the Garden of Eden when the serpent lied to Eve, will have its ultimate fulfillment when the Antichrist declares himself to be the Almighty God of this world.

Tragically, he will **succeed** in his efforts.

How can this BE?

The Bible says it will come about because of the religious and political unity already taking place through well-organized esoteric groups.

These include:
- Masonry
- New Agers

Antichrist Associates

- Liberal "Christians"
- Positive-thinking proponents
- Rosicrucians
- "Christian" psychologists
- Yoga practioners
- Silva Mind Control members
- Charismatic fringe movements
- *Some* Holistic Health Centers
- Pentecostal fringe movements
- Hindus
- Mormons
- Roman Catholic church

Symbols betray their true roots!

Satan will succeed because of the blatant efforts of the Freemasons to mislead their members by teaching the initiates that they are capable of becoming godlike through service in the Masons.

Satan also is seeing success through the Catholic Church because his symbols are worn by the Pope, the leader of the church, everytime he dons his papal tiara to grant a special audience.

But the greatest tragedy is that Satan is working even through Bible-oriented Christian church leaders who allow themselves to become involved in his work without realizing it.

For instance, there are charismatic leaders trying to force audience members to repeat words and babblings after them as a form of praying in tongues, or developing their "prayer language." The parallel to this exercise is the Hindu *mantra*.

Satan also is working through charismatic faith healers who lead audience members through emotionally charged, deceptive healing sessions. All of these examples reveal the hand of Lucifer through the joining together of certain esoteric organizations.

Gnosticism: alive and well

One common technique of deception used by these esoteric groups is gnosticism, the blending of true Bible teachings with occult doctrine.

This method, which distorts the full gospel message, is practiced a great deal within the groups exposed through this book.

Occult groups also are tied together through the use of similiar symbols.

What are these?

The papal tiara — also known as the "triple crown of godhood" by Masons and other religious groups, which is to be worn by the Antichrist

Antichrist Associates

in the end times — is merely one example.

Esoteric rituals

Similar rituals also are shared by the esoteric groups. The exorcism of salt and water rituals are shared by the Roman Catholic Church and a Jewish cult.

The Mormons and Freemasons also share similar rituals.

Esoteric groups have no regard for fundamental Bible principles and do not believe that Jesus Christ is Saviour and Lord. In fact, they are not bound by any Christian creed.

Satan knows his time is short.

Satan is exerting his power on earth like never before because he knows his time is short.

The second coming of Christ draws closer when Jesus will return to the planet and establish His Kingdom.

You will discover through this book that the most important action you or anyone else can take is to establish your relationship with the Lord Jesus Christ.

But, unfortunately ...

Regretably, many doctrines of "cosmic" Christianity have been spread in the name of the Saviour.

It is sometimes difficult to find a place where you can feel secure or sit before a pastor or evangelist and be sure you are receiving God's message clearly.

2

Warnings of the Antichrist

The Bible declares to us that in the end times one individual will arise and declare himself to be God.

The Bible calls this individual the "son of perdition" or —

The Antichrist

And the Bible tells us he will have associates all across the globe who will help deceive people into following him. The scriptures also teach that the Antichrist system will produce a pseudo-religion. This one-world religion will bring the allegiance of its masses to this man. The book of Revelation describes this scenario in chapter 13, verses one and two:

"And I stood upon the sand of the sea, and saw a beast rise up out of the sea, having seven heads and 10 horns, and upon his horns 10 crowns, and

upon his heads the name of blasphemy. The beast which I saw was like unto a leopard, and his feet were as the feet of a bear, and his mouth as the mouth of a lion, and the dragon gave him his power and his seat, and great authority." (Verses 1-2) (King James Version)

That is to say —

The devil himself will give this man all the power he has:

"And I saw one of his heads as it were wounded to death; and his deadly wound was healed: and all the world wondered after the beast." (Verse 3)

Some suggest that this individual will actually be killed and come back to life:

"They worshipped the dragon which gave power unto the beast: and they worshipped the beast, saying, 'Who is like unto the beast? who is able to make war with him?' And there was given unto him a mouth speaking great things, and blasphemies, and power was given unto him to continue 40 and two months.

(Three and one-half years.) (Verse 5)
"And he opened his mouth in blasphemy against God, to blaspheme His name, and His tabernacle and them that dwell in heaven." (Verse 6)

Power over all kindreds and tongues

The Antichrist will stand against the God of heaven and the followers of the Lord Jesus Christ.

"And it was given unto him to make war with the saints and to overcome them; and power was given him over all kindreds and tongues and nations." (Verse 7)

That is:

He's actually going to make war with those followers of the Lord Jesus Christ, to overcome them. We are seeing evidence of this in our country today through the outlawing of prayer in the schools and many other occurances too numerous to mention.

"And all that dwell upon the earth shall worship him, whose names are not written in the book of life of the Lamb slain from the foundation of the world. If any man have an ear, let him hear. He that leadeth into captivity go

leadeth into captivity shall go into captivity; he that killeth with the sword must be killed with the sword. Here is the patience and the faith of the saints. 'And I beheld another beast coming out of the earth; and he had two horns like a lamb and he spoke as a dragon.

"And he exerciseth all the power of the first beast before him and causes the Earth and them which dwell therein to worship the first beast, whose deadly wound was healed. And he doeth great wonders, so that he maketh fire come down from heaven on the earth in the sight of man." (Verses 8-13)

The Power Of The Antichrist

Antichrist will be given the ability to perform miracles and healing.

This will cause thousands throughout the world to pledge allegiance to him.

Thus, I am sure you can see, what an unhealthy climate that Charismatic television healer Richard Roberts created — and certainly what a dangerous precedent he set — when advocating "A Miracle Settles the Issue."

Miracles don't particularly prove anything, as the Word notes:

"And deceiveth them that dwell on the earth, by the means of those miracles which he had power to do in the sight of the beast; saying to them that dwell on the earth, that they should make an image to the beast which had the wound by a sword, and did live. And he had the power to give life unto the image of the beast, that the image of the beast should both speak, and cause that as many as would not worship the image of the beast should be killed.

The Word continues:

"And he causeth all, both small and great, rich and poor, free and bond, to receive a mark in their right hands, or in their foreheads; And that no man might buy or sell, save he that had the mark, or the name of the beast, or the number of his name.

"Here is wisdom: Let him that hath understanding count the number of the beast; for it is the number of a man; and his number is six hundred three-score and six." (Verses 14-18)

The book of Revelation predicts the coming of a one-world political and religious system. There will be tremendous unity.

Antichrist Associates

Unity across this **entire planet.**

Many have wondered:

How can this be? There are so many different opinions, especially politically and religiously. And how can unity come out of so many nations, so many languages, so many tongues, so many different religious groups?

Throughout this book we will expose the conspiracy that is spreading throughout our society and the entire world. We will give documentation showing that there are many well-known organizations working together to bring about this global community.

We will see how Satan is using mind control methods to unite his forces to gain power over all the earth. We will also equip the believer with the knowledge of the Bible which will enable him to stand against the false teachers of the day.

World unity under the Antichrist

The Epistle of Jude states:

"Beloved, when I gave all diligence to write unto you of the common salvation, it was needful for me to write unto you, and exhort you that

you should earnestly contend for the faith which was once delivered unto the saints. For there are cer-tain men crept in unawares, who were before of old ordained to this condemnation, ungodly men turn-ing the grace of our God into lasci-viousness, (lewdness) and denying the only Lord God, and our Lord Jesus Christ." (Verses 3-4)

Let No Man Deceive You

The Bible exhorts us to earnestly contend for the faith. Why? Because ungodly men have crept into the church. The Bible warns the believer to keep a vigilance for those who would pervert the teachings of God and the Bible. We must be on guard, especially in these ever-changing times for these wolves in sheep's clothing.

In addition

Another exhortation from the Bible is found in II Thessalonians 2:3-4, where the Apostle Paul tells us:

"Let no man deceive you by any means; for that day is not going to come, (referring to the rapture of the church) except there come a falling away first, (a falling away from the

Antichrist Associates

faith) and that man of sin be revealed, the son of perdition. Who opposeth and exalteth himself above all that is called God, or that is worshipped: so that he, as God, sitteth in the temple of God, shewing himself that he is God."

This is the big lie:

That any being can think he can be more powerful than or even *as powerful* as God our Creator.

It is incomprehensible to try to understand how a human being can become so egotistical as to think that he is Almighty God! But note again the apostle's words:

"Let no man deceive you by any means."

Lucifer and all his legions are deceiving believers, and non-believers alike by a variety of means. Paul wants us to be vigilant, alert to the ways and subtleties of our adversaries. They are commissioned to deceive. Unfortunately, they're experiencing great success.

Where did this lie begin?

It originated back in Genesis in the Garden of Eden. The Antichrist will be the ultimate manifestation of the serpent's lie which deceived Eve in the third chapter, verses 4 and 5:

"And the serpent said unto the woman, 'Ye shall not surely die. For God doth know that in the day ye eat thereof, then your eyes shall be opened, and ye shall be as gods, knowing good and evil.'"

The serpent, of course, is the devil, Lucifer and this grand lie will have its final fulfillment in the person of the Antichrist, when he declares himself God. Lucifer has planned toward this end since the first deception in the garden.

Anti-Biblical Societies

Is there anyone today who actually teaches that we can become gods?
Yes!
Incredibly, they are all around us!
There are many religious and seemingly non-religious organizations which teach that man can move into godhood.
Some even believe that they are already gods.
One example of such an organization is Freemasonry.

Antichrist Associates

The following is an excerpt from *The Lost Keys of Freemasonry*, a book written by Manley P. Hall, a 33rd-degree Mason, who notes on page 92:

The triple crown of godhood?

"Man is a god in the making. And as in the mystic myths of Egypt, on the potter's wheel, he is being molded. When his light shines out to lift and preserve all things, he receives the triple crown of godhood."

This clearly reveals:

Freemasonry teaches that members can become gods. However, other writings by other members declare that they **are** God when they discover this within themselves.

This intimation can be clearly seen in George H. Steinmetz's book *The Royal Arch, Its Hidden Meaning*, on page 98:

The candidate is made to state "I AM hath sent me unto you." Thus, the first requirement must be "to be sent by God." If one claims "to be sent by God," the very claim is tacit admission of belief in the God that sent him.

If one pauses a moment to

consider what he actually claims when he declares "I AM," he realizes it is a statement of his own existence, his consciousness thereof and an assertion of divinity, for only Deity and man made in His image can assert "I AM."

What does this show us?

This clearly reveals the belief in Freemasonry that they are attributing to themselves deity.

This becomes equally as clear when we read on in page 123:

*Here is set forth a truth which the Bible reiterates again and again: "The kingdom of heaven is within" — "The kingdom of heaven is nigh" — "The word is ever nigh thee, even in thy mouth and in thy heart" — constant, repetitious reminders that man is divine and the place to seek that divinity is **within himself.***

Divinity within ourselves?

This information is merely being served as a form of education for those in Biblical Christianity who do not believe that "man is divine."

Freemasons have a right to believe whatever they believe.

Unfortunately, many sincere

Antichrist Associates

Christians who are members of this organization are not aware of the anti-Christian elements involved.

Finally,

On page 133, we read:

The Hebrew (Hebrew characters), translated Jehovah, denotes "He who was, He who is, and He who will be." This is Deity. Ponder over the fact that we are informed: "Man is made in the image and likeness of his Creator" and the first faint flush of dawn will permeate our mental horizon. Another intimation is contained in the answer to the question: "Are you a Royal Arch Mason?"

If asked "Are You a Master Mason," the natural response would be the affirmative, "I AM."

Read on:

Few realize the double import of this answer. It informs the inquirer that one is a Master Mason, but it is likewise a declaration of one's very existence. To state, "I am" is, in effect, a claim to consciousness — "I BE" ... Each individual must discover it for himself. Divinity is within, not without.

When the Jewish people in Jesus' day realized that Jesus was ascribing to himself Deity, they wanted to stone him for blasphemy. They believed only God was divine — and rightly so.

Historic Christianity believes the very same thing. To belong to such an organization would be totally out of order for the Bible-believing Christian.

When the author stated that few realized the double import of this answer, "I AM," when asked if he was a Master Mason, he is correct. I know of many Freemasons who believe in and love the Lord Jesus Christ very much, and certainly do not realize the import contained in this reply.

Remember, only God is "I AM."

In contrast to the esoteric method of intentionally deceiving the under-lings, Biblical Christianity commands its teachers to declare plainly the truth of God to everyone and never to to do anything craftily or deceitfully. We are to proclaim what God has promised in a clear and open fashion.

God desires that all have the opportunity to make an intelligent decision about why they chose to follow or not to follow the Lord Jesus Christ.

Antichrist Associates

He sets two roads before us:

One that leads to eternal life with Christ Jesus and the other that leads to eternal damnation.

Link Between Masons and Catholics

Most people are under the impression that Freemasonry and Roman Catholicism are diametrically opposed to each other. Nothing could be further from the truth.

One of the links between these organizations is the "triple crown of godhood" to which we referred earlier. The Pope, leader of the Catholic religion, traditionally wears what is called the papal tiara, containing three layers of crowns on one headdress.

The book, *The Lost Keys Of Freemasonry* describes the Master Mason as looking forward to the time he will receive the triple crown of godhood, as we mentioned previously.

Additionally:

Another link between the Roman religion and the esoteric world can also be seen when the Pope is functioning in an official capacity.

When the Pope bestows his blessing upon an audience, he cups his in a peculiar manner that would not be natural, but an especially designed form. It seems that this gesture is parallel to a form found in the occult.

Look for yourself:

In a book entitled *Ancient Pagan and Modern Christian Symbolism,* written by Thomas Inman, I recently discovered a page filled with esoteric symbols. To my amazement, there was an illustration of the Latin symbol for the hand of God. Comparing the illustration with pictures of the Pope of Rome when he bestows his blessing with his hand, I discovered they are precisely the same.

On the same page ...

There with other esoteric symbols is also the Greek form of the hand of God. The coincidence deepened when I realized that Latin is the official language of the Roman Catholic mass.

This Latin form of "the hand of God" along with the triple crown of godhood worn by the Roman pontiff seemed to declare the very same thing the Master Masons do.

Again, one must realize that symbols are extremely important to esoteric organizations. These are fraternal symbols familiar to those adepts and sages of the various occultic groups around the world and they communicate through these symbols.

Weird? Silly?

This all may sound absurd and bizarre to those who belong to some of these organizations — and rightly so. The reason being, they have not been informed of the meaning and interpretations behind the symbology.

However, all one has to do to corroborate the meanings is to do some simple investigation.

Allow me to share my discoveries when I did just that.

3

Gnosticism: Blending Occult and Biblical Christianity

How did it happen?

How did demonic beliefs, practices, rituals and symbols gain acceptance in religious organizations and the Church?

When did this happen?

Yesterday?

The 1800s?

Maybe 90 A.D., as soon at the Apostles were dead and buried?

No, Satan's perversions have crept in from all sides ever since the Apostle Peter's first altar call on the Day of Pentecost. Paul warned us to be eternally vigilant as he denounced evil already tainting congregations — such as the evangelistic apathy at Laodicea, the drunkenness at Corinth's communion services and the serious factionalism elsewhere.

The pure, white walls of Jesus Christ's new Church quickly developed water stains, mildew, cracks and graffiti. But since it happened gradually, nobody became alarmed.

Well, there are historical exceptions.

As if leaping up from a nightmare, Martin Luther suddenly began denouncing corrupt and ungodly church practices threatening the church of the Middle Ages. There, believers were permitted to pay cash "penance" in advance before committing various sins, for example. Yet, they were forbidden from reading the Scriptures.

Then in the 1700s, such firebrands as Jonathan Edwards reminded the docile, sleepy church of the anger of an ignored God.

Yet, despite such historic revivals as the Great Awakening, Satan has continued to divide, weaken and corrupt the Church.

It is frightening to see the ease at which Satan has infiltrated Christian theology, liturgy, philosophy and psychology with cosmic disinformation, lies and confusion.

Standing back and looking at the damage, I find myself filled with incredulity.

It seems so incomprehensible. How could Christians be so gullible?

How can we be seduced so easily?

How can sincere Bible believers have been beguiled into accepting spurious, destructive, evil "Christian" teachings whose roots reach not back to Peter, Paul, James and John — and to our Lord — but deep into Satan's insidious occult?

John saw the threat back in the very first days of the Church — and cautioned the faithful against what was then called Gnosticism.

Look at his warning in I John 4:

Beloved, believe not every spirit, but try the spirits whether they are of God; because many false prophets are gone out into the world. Hereby know ye the Spirit of God: Every spirit that confesseth that Jesus Christ is come in the flesh is of God:

And every spirit that confesseth not that Jesus Christ is come in the flesh is not of God: and this is that spirit of antichrist, whereof ye have heard that it should come; and even now already is it in the world. (Verses 1-3)

In II John, he was more to the point:

... Many deceivers are entered into the world who confess not that Jesus

Christ is come in the flesh. This is a deceiver and an antichrist. Look to yourselves, that we lose not those things which we have wrought, but that we receive a full reward.

Whosoever transgresseth, and abideth not in the doctrine of Christ, hath not God. He that abideth in the doctrine of Christ, he hath both the Father and the Son.

If there come any unto you, and bring not this doctrine, receive him not into your house, neither bid him God speed: For he that biddeth him God speed is partaker of his evil deeds. (Verses 7-11)

Today — just as back then — Gnostics do not look at Jesus Christ the way you and I do.

They degrade his significance.

They look at Him as nothing more than a Master Mason, an Ascended Master, a wise teacher but lower than the principle gurus of the eastern religions. They consider him a great yogi, sometimes even a god, but not Almighty God. The Lord Jesus ends up as an also-ran of the underling gods.

And so they ask you to search for the true god within you, which you and I know is Luciferic. On page 1,240 of *The International Standard Bible Encyclopedia*, we read the following:

Gnosticism may be described generally as the fantastic product of the blending of certain Christian ideas — particularly that of redemption through Christ — with speculations and imaginings derived from a medley of sources (Greek, Jewish, Parsic; philosophies, religions, theosophies, mysteries) in a period when the human mind was in a kind of ferment, and when opinions of every sort were jumbled together in an unimaginable welter. It involves, as the name denotes, a claim to "knowledge," knowledge of a kind of which the ordinary believer was incapable, and in the possession of which "salvation" in the full sense consisted. This knowledge of which the Gnostic boasted, related to the subjects ordinarily treated of in religious philosophy; Gnosticism was a species of religious philosophy.

Homogenizing truth and lies

This blending to which the author refers plays a great part in these esoteric black magic and witchcraft movement as well. There is the law of duality that prevails in these esoteric groups and their attempt to create the "blend" between the two opposites. One example of this can be found in the symbol of the two triangles depicting a union, of opposites which can also symbolize a sexual union.

Dr. W.B. Robertson on page 1,247 of the *International Standard Bible Encyclopedia* states the following philosopher's view of man and God and his own personal opinion of their view:

God and man are one, and God all men, and all men God, and the whole universe God eternally thinking in the process of development and that or something like it, is Hegelianism [the philosopher's position]. I feel in studying this philosophy, as Baron Humboldt says he felt, when he experienced the first shock of an earthquake. I feel a dreadful sense of restlessness and insecurity. The ground seems to give way beneath, and the earth and the heaven to dissolve, the universe becomes a dream, a myth.

However, the Bible says,
"Professing themselves to be wise, they become fools."

Here's what I Timothy 6:20 advises:
"Keep that which is committed to thy trust, avoiding profane and vane babblings and oppositions of science — or knowledge — falsely so called."

Avoid these teachers, Paul said.
Don't let them into your home, urged John. Don't even bid them God speed.

Shun them, the Bible cautions.

Gnosticism wants to blend Biblical Christianity with Esoteria — and produce a watered-down Gospel that offers no threat to the forces of hell and their Antichrist.

And, as you can see, this is no new thing.

But just as the early church had to be warned, wary and watchful — so must we today.

More than ever before!
While I was in South Africa on a series of meetings, a missionary asked me to review a book entitled *Cults and The Occult* which explained various elements of black magic and white magic. The missionary had learned from the book that a great deal of sorcery, demonism and witchcraft was indeed pervading the country.

Antichrist Associates

As I turned the pages, it was interesting to see the various esoteric religious movements proclaiming their various evil teachings under a variety of guises. Each had its own symbols and rituals, yet their common hellish roots were obvious.

Straight from the pit, that is.

Having seen symbols of the triple crown, I came across a picture of the Great Seal of Solomon, which is also referred to as the Double Triangle of Solomon. A more common reference to the basic seal is the Star of David, a prominent emblem on the Israeli flag. At the top of the Star of David was the face of a man wearing — to my surprise — a triple crown.

This symbolism is part of the Kabala, the esoteric side of Judaism. This occultism has nothing to do with Biblical Judaism, of which the Lord Jesus Christ and Biblical Christianity are a part.

It's pure occultism.

What this did was to reveal to me how extensive this networking within the occult really is.

This is precisely the heart of what the New Age Movement is all about. In assessing the present situation in Christendom, Gnosticism becomes more visible and the need to try the spirits becomes more acute.

We live under grace

When the Lord Jesus Christ came, of course He did away with religion, and so He implemented the new system we're in today, and this is Biblical Christianity, the "Age of Grace. "

It's interesting that the more you research, the more you see the New Age thread of Gnosticism woven through churches and organizations worldwide. There is a tremendous reason behind all of this, and it is of high importance that born-again believers get the right picture of this potent anti-Christian influence.

In fact, this ancient Gnosticism has many faces today — appearing in religious groups that blend the Bible with the occult. The Kabala even quotes John 1:1:

"In the beginning was the word, and the word was with God, and the word was God."

Now this is what they refer to as the incomprehensible god, or *ain soph.* They say that first came part of the Jewish scriptures known as the Torah. The Torah was the word. According to thm, God came after the word.

This is an example of Gnosticism.

It is *false, twisted* teaching.

This type of falsehood is prevalent among esoteric religions. You will find it in Hinduism. You will find it in the Jewish Kabala. You will find this in the dogma of Freemasonry.

You will find it in black magic.

It's a concoction of lies and truth.

The word of John 1:1 is referred to as the incomprehensible god. We are told that we can understand him only by mixing in other "revelation." Actually, this is none other than Lucifer disguising himself as "the word" in his attempt to deceive people into thinking that he has been exalted above Jesus Christ, as God.

The origin of the triple crown

The Freemasons and Catholics are strongly tied together, and it's by design and not by chance.

We have presented the uniqueness of the papal tiara, which is in fact a triple crown. But what is the origin of this papal crown? We talked about the triple crown of godhood in Freemasonry and the Kabala, the Jewish esoteric movement. But where did the triple crown come from?

What is its origin?

You will discover that when the papal tiara is displayed in a publication, you will generally find the two crossed "keys of Saint Peter" in the same illustration or near it. The Roman Catholic Church suggests these are the keys to the kingdom of Heaven that Christ gave to Peter.

Or are they, really?

A clue to the possible origin of the papal tiara and the crossed keys can be found on page 29 of a book called *Isis Unveiled* published by the Theosophical University Press, an esoteric organization:

The very apostolic designation of Peter is from the mysteries. The supreme pontiff bore the title Peter, or "interpreter."

The text goes on to say that "no apostle Peter was ever in Rome, however." Most Protestant theologians and some Roman Catholic scholars are in agreement that Peter was never in Rome. Hence, he could not have been the first pope as insisted by the Roman religion.

Just what was Peter's assignment?
Peter is referred to in the Bible as the *apostle to the circumcision,* the Jews. The apostle Paul was called the *apostle of the uncircumcision,* the Gentiles. This book by an esoteric organization agrees that Peter was never in Rome.

Page 30 of *Isis Unveiled* states:
No apostle Peter was ever in Rome; but the Pope, seizing the sceptre of the Pontifex Maximus, the keys of Janus and Kubele, and adorning his Christian head with the cap of the Magna Mater, copied from that of the tiara of Brahmatma, the Supreme Pontiff of the Initiates of old India, became the successor of the Pagan high priest, the real Peter-Roma, or Petroma ... the tiara of the Pope is also a perfect copy of that of the Dalai-Lama of Tibet.

According to one French scholar, Jacolliot, the two crossed keys also have their origin in the east.

He claims to have translated every ancient palm-leaf manuscript given to him by the Brahmans of the pagodas.

The importance of 'aum'

He says:

*Whomsoever among these initiates revealed to profane a single one of the truths even the smallest of the secrets entrusted to his care, was put to death. He who received the confidence had to share his fate. "Finally, to crown this able system," says Jacolliot, "there existed a word still more superior to the mysterious monosyllable — **aum**, and which rendered him who came into the possession of its key nearly the equal of Brahma himself. The Brahm-atma alone possessed this key, and transmitted it in a sealed casket to his successor.*

This unknown word, of which no human power could, even today, when the Brahmanical authority has been crushed under the Mongolian and European invasions, today when each pagoda has its Brahm-atma, force the disclosure, was engraved in a golden triangle and preserved in a sanctuary *of the temple of Asgartha, whose Brahm-atma alone held the keys. He also bore upon his tiara **two crossed keys** supported by two kneeling Brahmans, symbols of the precious deposit of which he had the keeping.*

Golden sun on the altar

In possible contrast to the Roman Catholic monstrance, the unit which contains "the host," the ingredient in communion can also be found on this same page where we read:

*This word and this triangle were engraved upon the table of the ring that this religious chief wore as one of the signs of his dignity; it was also framed in a **golden sun on the altar** [emphasis ours] where every morning the Supreme Pontiff offered the sacrifice of the sarvameda, or sacrifice to all the forces of nature.*

The Catholic monstrance is designed like a golden sunburst.

"This word" referred to as engraved upon the tablet of the ring that the religious head wore is in contrast to the "word" of the Kabalists who perverted "The Word" in John 1:1. The Word referred to in

John 1:1 is in reference to the person of the Lord Jesus Christ:

In the beginning was the word, and the word was with God, and the word was God.

Back to the triple crown:

Finally *Isis Unveiled* gives us yet another illustration of the ancestry of the triple crown on page 94:

If we would find the model of the Papal tiara, we must search the annals of the ancient Assyrian tablets.

We invite the reader to give his attention to Dr. Inman's illustrated work Ancient Pagan and Modern Christian Symbolism.

On page 64, he will readily recognize the headgear of the successor of Saint Peter in the coiffeur worn by god or angels in ancient Assyria, "where it appears crowned by an emblem of the male trinity" (the Christian Cross).

In closing ...

We conclude this chapter with the statement made on page 32 of *Isis Unveiled* which in this context takes on new importance:

Antichrist Associates

> *And will the Catholics still maintain that it was the Brahmans of 4,000 years ago who copied the ritual, symbols and dress of the Roman Pontiffs?*

4

Cosmic Christianity

The Luciferic perversion of the Gospel goes deep — much deeper than many of us want to admit.

Satan's claws clutch the Church in an insidious grip that threatens to mute the Good News.

Our research reveals extensive inroads made by these esoteric movements into traditional Christianity. When one investigates the rituals performed, added proof is found that seemingly opposing organizations are actually walking down the very same path.

For example:

Isis Unveiled provides some interesting parallels between some of the rituals of Kabalistic and Roman Catholic religions. One of the Kabalistic rituals cited is called the Exorcism of salt. This Kabalistic ceremony goes as follows:

Antichrist Associates

The Priest-Magician blesses the salt, and says, "Creature of salt, in thee may remain the **wisdom** *(of God); and may it preserve from all corruption our minds and bodies. Through Hochmael (Hebrew characters, God of wisdom), and the power of Ruach Hochmael (Spirit of the Holy Ghost) may the Spirits of matter (bad spirits) before it recede ... Amen.*

So, look at this:

The Roman Catholic exorcism of salt is as follows:

The Priest blesses the salt and says: "Creature of Salt, I exorcise thee in the name of the living God ... become the health of the soul and of the body! Everywhere where thou art thrown may unclean spirit be put to flight ... Amen."

Now, we will cite only the opening of the next two comparative rituals:

Kabalistic Exorcism of Water (and Ashes):

"Creature of the Water, I exorcise thee ... by the three names ..."

The Roman Catholic Exorcism of Water:

"Creature of the water, in the name of the Almighty God, the Father,

the Son, and the Holy Ghost ... be exorcised."

Kabalistic Exorcism of an Elemental Spirit:

"Serpent, in the name of Tetragammaton, the Lord; He commands thee, by the angel and the lion."

Roman Catholic Exorcism of the Devil:

"O Lord, let him who carries along with him the terror, flee, struck in his turn by terror and defeated. O thou, who are the Ancient Serpent."

There are many more striking parallels between these organizations than time and space would allow us. Sufficient is the proof that cosmic parallels are extremely common among them that they are more than coincidental.

The parallels extend beyond this

They can be found in white magic movements as well as in cosmic movements which would seem to be very far from the ones cited here. But a simple investigation of their teachings reveals the affinity among them.

In my research I also discovered many striking similarities between the two organizations, not merely on the phrases used but also of the ceremonies involved.

This is more proof that these cosmic rituals actually permeate all of these various religious organizations of the world which seem to oppose one another but are in reality one and the same. They are also motivated by an identical spirit.

Title for nuns has roots in occult

According to the Theosophical University Press, "the title of nun is actually an Egyptian word."

Nuns are women who comprise a special order or service within the Roman Catholic Church.

You see nuns all the time.

But the title itself is an Egyptian word.

The Catholics did not even take the trouble of translating the Greek word "nonna."

This, my dear friend, is simply cosmic Christianity or Gnosticism: the blending of paganism and Christianity.

When you do that it becomes part of the occult, and the power and force behind it is not God.

Mormon-Mason similarities

Astonishing similarities have also been discovered between the Mormon Church — formally known as the Church of Jesus Christ of Latter Day Saints — and Freemasonry.

Vows taken by those participating in the temple rituals of these organizations are identical.

In presenting the oaths made by these initiates, we want to remember the secrecy sworn to by initiates of the third and supreme degree of the religion of ancient India where the Brahm-atma was the guardian of the esoteric mysteries.

Secrecy bound by death

If these initiates were to betray a single truth of the smallest significance, they were to be put to death. This severe penalty is also part of the oaths taken in Freemasonry and Temple Mormonism.

An oath taken from page 18 of Temple Mormonism says:

We, and each of us, covenant and promise that we will not reveal any of the secrets. of this, the first token of the Aaronic priesthood, with its accompanying name, sign or penalty.

Antichrist Associates

Should we do so, we agree that our throats be cut from ear to ear, and our tongues be torn out by their roots.

Similarly:

Such an oath is given in Free-masonry. Upon receiving his first degree, a Mason states:

I bring myself under no less penalty than that of having my throat cut across, my tongue torn out by its roots and my body buried in the rough sand of the sea at the low-water mark."

No mere idle recreation

The oaths reveal the sinister force and common threat of unity behind these organizations.

Added to this, we recall the Biblical command in the Book of James 5:12 which clearly forbids us to swear:

But above all things, my brethren, swear not. Swear not; neither by heaven, nor by the earth, or by anything under the earth, or by any other oath, lest you fall into condemnation.

Our Lord Jesus also instructed his disciples in Matthew 5:34:

But I say unto you, swear not at all; neither by heaven; for it is God's throne."

That is a simple statement that can be understood by anyone.

It is sad that Christians belonging to Freemasonry will totally disregard, some unknowingly, the command of the Saviour and submit to a command that seems to have been given by Satan.

Examine the passage designated as "Moses 5:29" in one of the extra-biblical sacred texts of the Mormon church, a book called *The Pearl Of Great Price:*

"And Satan said unto Cain, 'Swear unto me by your throat, and if you tell it, you shall die. And swear your brethren by their heads, and by the living god, that they tell it not. For if they tell it, they shall surely die.' "

Though the Mormon religion claims to believe the Bible, note their clear disregard for the commands of the Bible as they implement a command by the devil. The devil issues the command to Cain, the evil brother who murdered Abel. He killed his brother not because of any wrong Abel did to him, but because he was envious of God's respect for Abel.

Look at what the Bible really says.

The respect came because Abel offered the sacrifice God asked for. It was very simple. Cain refused to offer the prescribed sacrifice and chose to offer his own.

This jealousy, which consumed Cain, is the very same sadistic force that will drive Lucifer's initiates to kill God's people during the great tribulation period.

Is Freemasonry a religion?

Ed Decker of Saints Alive in Jesus Ministries, cites an article in his booklet entitled *The Question of Freemasonry* that provides us with information on some of the deception practiced by this organization. Mr. Decker quotes a newspaper article called, *Freemasonry — A Way of Life*, which appeared in many metropolitan areas. He quotes the article as stating:

*Masonry is **not** a religion in any sense of the word, yet it is religious. Church membership is not a require-*

*ment, yet membership in **any** church is no bar to admission. There is nothing in the requirements of Masonry to prevent a Catholic, a Mohammedan, a Jew, a Buddhist, a Protestant, a Mormon or any member of any religion from becoming a member.*

However, according to the Encyclopedia of Freemasonry:

Every Masonic temple is a temple of religion, and its teachings are instructions in religion (page 213). It is the universal, eternal, immutable religion, such as God planted in the heart of universal humanity. No creed has ever been long-lived that was not built on this foundation. It is the base and they [all the other religions] are the superstructure.

On the other hand:
The Bible has something different to say in regard to this in I Corinthians 3:11 where it declares to us that man can lay no other foundation than that which has been put in place by Jesus Christ.

He, not Freemasonry, is the foundation.

Another common characteristic

among esoteric religions is that they are not bound by creeds. One statement to this effect is contained on page 65 of *The Lost Keys of Freemasonry* by Manley Hall.

"The true mason is not creed bound. He realizes with divine illumination of his lodge that as a Mason his religion must be universal. Christ, Buddha, Mohammed, the name means little, because he recognizes only the light and not the bearer [This person, this true Mason] worships at every shrine, bows before every altar, whether in temple, mosque or cathedral — realizing with this truer understanding the oneness of all spiritual truth."

So, I ask you:

If Christ means little to true Masons, why do good Christians belong to the group?

Admittedly, there are hundreds and perhaps thousands of wonderful, godly men who are Freemasons. I personally know of several Bible-preaching pastors who are Masons.

This being the case, why would these people who dearly love the Lord Jesus Christ and His Bible, belong to an organization where the name of Christ means little?

This is difficult to comprehend until you become aware of a common principle in esoteric organizations.

That is: they deliberately conceal the truth *about themselves* — and not only from outsiders, but from initiates and other members not in leadership.

Lost Keys of Freemasonry notes:

Masonry, like all the religions, all the mysteries ... conceals its secrets from all except the adepts and sages, or the elect. And they use false explanations and false interpretations of its symbols to ... mislead those who deserve only to be mislead. To conceal the truth, which it calls light, from them and to draw them away from it. Truth is not for those who are unworthy, or unable to receive it or would pervert it.

This is the reason that so many are misled. They are led as lambs to the slaughter. Many of them are sincere, godly men and women who actually are deceived into thinking they are doing something good for God.

Yet, all the time they are doing nothing more than promoting the cause of Lucifer, the one who wants to exalt himself above God.

Indeed, their participation actually leads them farther away from understanding the joy of really walking with Christ and experiencing the freedom of forgiveness of personal sin.

Beware of counterfeit lookalikes!

An esoteric organization can never bring to its members the grandeur of the person of the Lord Jesus Christ, the God of creation, the God of redemption, the One who loved us so much that He would die for us. He took upon His body our personal sins to pay our penalty.

But many are deceived.

The deception of sincere Christians can be called nothing more than a deep tragedy.

Others, in New Age groups, also are deceived into thinking that they are performing righteous acts in furthering the work of God.

What lies ahead for them?

A forgiving God?

Or a sobering realization on Judgment Day that they failed to search the Scriptures or seek the Lord's will and have been blindly preparing the world for the reign of the Antichrist?

 5 *World Unity*
Under Satan's Power

What does the Bible say about this Satanic plot to subvert the Gospel, infiltrate the Church and to divide and confuse God's elect?

Believe it or not, it's all foretold

Lucifer's plan to bring our planet under a one-world political and religious system is articulately described throughout the Bible and especially in the book of Revelation.

Bible students are aware that the Antichrist himself will rule this world for seven terrible years.

The Tribulation approaches!

As we near the dawning of this Aquarian Age — as it is referred to by New Agers, we certainly will be witnessing the beginning of sorrows and the staging that must precede the actual Tribulation itself.

Antichrist Associates

To illustrate a case in point, we refer to an article which appeared in the July 1986 *Bible in the News* monthly publication of the Southwest Radio Church of the Air.

On page 12 of that publication, reference was made to the April 1986 issue of *Science 86* magazine, which carried an article entitled "The Supermarket Snoop."

Numbers at the supermarket

The article informs us that some 2,500 shoppers in approximately 20 cities have volunteered to show a numbered card each time they shop. They were to record everything from purchases to choices made.

Southwest Radio Church has been in the forefront for several decades providing daily insights into prophetic indicators such as this — events which the Bible predicted would come to pass during the latter stages of this dispensation.

The Bible tells us:

The nearer we come to the beginning of the Tribulation when the Antichrist will control the world, the more he will intensify his efforts.

His influence will be such that

Jesus poses the question, will be faith be found on the earth when He returns. We read of this in Revelation 12:9-12.

Wanted: those who love not their lives

And the great dragon was cast out, that old serpent, called the Devil, and Satan, which deceiveth the whole world: he was cast out into the earth, and his angels were cast out with him. And I heard a loud voice saying in heaven, 'Now is come salvation and strength, and the kingdom of our God, and the power of his Christ; for the accuser of our brethren is cast down, overcome by the blood of the lamb, and by the word of their testimony; and they loved not their lives unto the death. Therefore rejoice, ye heavens and ye that dwell in them. Woe to the inhabitants of the earth, and of the sea! for the devil is come down unto you, having great wrath, because he knoweth that he hath but a short time.

Be wary! Be watchful!

In light of these ominous thunderings from the forces of darkness, we want to keep in the forefront the exhortation of 2 Thessalonians 2:3 to be vigilant and not allowing anyone to deceive us by any means.

Satan will utilize any means available to him to lead as many as he can away from God.

Why does he have such wrath?

Because he knows his time is short. The second coming of Christ draws closer when Jesus will return to this planet and establish His kingdom.

Satan knows his time is very short

That's why he's intensifying his efforts and strengthening those working for him. And we already know there are many organizations — seemingly different — working together for the glory of Lucifer.

However, born-again believers must remember the apostle Paul's warning in II Thessalonians 2:3:

"Let no man deceive you by any means."

Satan is going to use any means available to him to deceive you and lead you astray.

Again we cite the Masons as an example of how Lucifer works through international esoteric organizations.

This group, like other occults, uses gnosticism, ancient and mysterious rituals and even blatant deceit to promote the efforts of Satan.

Satan's work via Masons & Mormons

Interestingly enough, even though there is a special intent, as we previously noted, by Freemasonry to deliberately mislead many within their organization, there is also some very plain teaching available to the public which clearly shows the power base.

By their own admission, the Masons are an esoteric organization, a mystical, secretive occult. And so we — especially the born-again believers — want to beware of Lucifer's work through this group.

Lucifer is anxious

He is eager to usher in this New Age, this great tribulation period when he will rule and reign through the Antichrist upon Earth.

Throughout this book we have seen bonds between Freemasonry and Roman Catholicism which strengthen the work of Satan in this world by developing a worldwide political and religious unity. But we also must look at the work of the Mormons, who have a similar goal of a global, one-world government.

For example, on page 48 of Manly P. Hall's *Lost Keys of Freemasonry*, we read of the power that is working through them:

> *When the Mason ... has learned the mystery of his craft ... the seething energies of Lucifer are in his hands and before he may step onward and upward, he must prove his ability to properly apply [this] energy.*

Nothing can be clearer than this:

These people are nothing more than **Luciferians.** They actually believe Satan's spirit is flowing through them, and they are proud of it. This kind of teaching is something which pervades all of these esoteric religions.

However, the born-again believer still has to wonder why these people would bring themselves under such bondage.

It is this common denominator that I believe to be moving the Roman Catholic religion and Freemasonry in collaborating to bring about this ages-old desire of the Aquarian Age of Antichrist, the New Order. Ed Decker and Dave Hunt mentioned in their book *The God Makers* an article by John J. Stewart, a Mormon writer:

The prophet established a confidential counsel of 50 or "Ytfif," ("Fifty" spelled backwards) comprised of both Mormon and non-Mormons to help attend to temporal matters, which includes the eventual development of a one-world government, and this is in harmony with preparatory plans for the second advent of the Saviour."

Note they are working with non-Mormons, to include the eventual development of a one-world government. I personally know of no orthodox Christian denomination with a committed Biblical position that would be working for a global government.

The mention of the preparatory plans for the second advent of the Saviour is especially noteworthy for the dedicated Bible student. I know that no orthodox student of the Bible would ever be making preparatory plans with those of the Mormon religion for the second advent of the

Savior. There is no common ground whatsoever between Orthodox Biblical Christianity and Mormonism. So with which non-Mormons would the confidential Council of Fifty be making these preparatory plans?

First of all:

In answer to the second advent of the Saviour, there are many Bible scholars who speculate the Antichrist will be Judas Iscariot.

According to 2 Thessalonians, the second coming of Christ Jesus will be preceded by a period of great tribulation led by one referred to as "the son of perdition." There are varied opinions as to who will be the Antichrist.

But some Bible scholars believe the Antichrist will actually be coming for the second time.

***That* man. Who is he?**

The Bible refers to "**that** man of sin" not "**a** man of sin," which they believe might refer back to the one who was previously identified by that title. Because of this and many of the parallels between Christ and the Antichrist, some suspect it could be possible for Judas Iscariot to return a second time, hence the reference to the second coming of the Saviour by the Mormon religion, which is purely an occult religion.

Indeed:

To be sure, there are several opinions on who the Antichrist may or may not be among orthodox Bible students.

We merely bring this possibility to your attention because of the Mormon writer's reference to the preparatory plans for the second coming.

Southwest Radio Church of the Air in their commentary on the Book of Revelation states that more knowledge was given to John than to any other apostle in regard to the Antichrist.

Also:

Also, he refers to this satanic force throughout his epistles.

SWRC suggests that if we correlate the Word of God by reading in sequence the Gospel of John, we could arrive at an interesting conclusion.

The scriptures indicate that the wicked one may very well be Judas Iscariot, the apostle who betrayed Jesus at the time of our Saviour's death.

Antichrist Associates

Now, of course, no one can be dogmatic on this position, because no one knows precisely who the Antichrist might be.

Who are the Mormons expecting?

We bring this up because the Mormons state they are looking for the second advent of *their* saviour. If this is true, then it can refer only to the one who came the first time, the first Antichrist, the first one who betrayed the Lord Jesus Christ and that was Judas.

John 17 refers to Judas as "the son of perdition."

The son of perdition

It is clear that more knowledge was given to John than any other apostle in regards to the Antichrist, and he refers to the satanic force throughout his epistles.

Now if we correlate the Word of God by reading in sequence the gospel of John, then the first epistle of John and then the Revelation of John the Divine, it is difficult for us to arrive at any other conclusion but that perhaps Judas himself will be reincarnated upon Earth as the Antichrist.

But we must remember that the Mormons are working with non-Mormons to usher in this new age of cosmic Christianity.

I believe the Mormons are working with the Freemasons, the Roman Catholics and other esoteric organizations.

How? Why? ... you may be asking

Outwardly they may not seem to have much in common.

However, more and more you see them coming out in the open and acknowledging one common purpose.

Consider this:

In a publication prepared by Benedictines for Peace, Pax Christi USA, a publication called *The Challenge of Peace: God's Promise and Our Response, Pastoral Letter of U.S. Catholic Bishops,* there is some extremely interesting information.

It could lead a person to speculate upon a possible collaboration between the Roman Catholic church and the Mormons' Church of Jesus Christ of Latter Day Saints on the preparation of plans for a one-world government.

On page 45 of the booklet, we read:

Antichrist Associates

> In the past 20 years, Catholic teaching has become increasingly specific about the content of these international rights and duties. In 1963, **Peace on Earth** sketched the political and legal order among states. In 1967, **The Development of Peoples** elaborated on order of economic rights and duties. In 1979, Pope John Paul articulated the human rights basis of international relations in his address to the United Nations. These documents and others which build upon them outlined a moral order of international relations, i.e., how the international community should be organized ... While not ignoring present geopolitical realities, one of the primary functions of Catholic teaching on world order has been to point the way toward a more integrated international system. In analyzing this path toward world order, the category increasingly used in Catholic moral teaching (and, more recently, in the social sciences also) is the interdependence of the world today.

One Catholic world?

The Roman Catholic religion readily acknowledges that a new world order is one of the primary functions of Catholic teaching. This being the case and their commitment to the theological unity leaves one little doubt but to believe there is a collaboration of the Elect of both organizations in the preparations of plans for the new global society.

Want to join up?

On page 46 was a questionnaire with this leading question, "If you are interested in working for a new world order, a group to contact is **Global Education Associates**" with an address in East Orange, New Jersey.

Give us your opinion ...

It went on to ask the questionnaire recipient to respond to several bizarre statements — including the following:

• *My country should be willing to sacrifice some sovereignty for the sake of international cooperation.*
• *I would not be willing to be governed by a world parliament representing other races in the majority.*
• *I would prefer to be a citizen of the world rather than of just one country.*
• *I do not have and would not care*

to have a world flag to fly on my premises.

These odd statements are only a few of those that were offered.

What purpose were they to serve?

I think you can guess.

I can assure you that I know of no orthodox, Bible-oriented church involved in anything resembling this.

And I can tell you the secret source:

Bible scholars of all the major denominations have presented well-documented studies detailing the scenario of the one-world government of the Antichrist.

Now, look at this:

An international community?

In this same pastoral letter of the United States Roman Catholic Bishops, the church emphasized the need for "an international community."

The publication, entitled *Reflection On Guide, the Challenge of Peace, God's Promise and Our Response*, shows how this bishops' council is actually working with other esoteric groups to bring about a one-world religious and political system:

"These documents and others, which build upon them, outlined a moral order for international relations — that is, how the international community should be organized."

Moral order in world relations

Here we find Roman Catholic bishops, men who are not even politicians, stating how a moral order of international relations should be structured.

They say in the letter,

"While not ignoring present geopolitical realities, one of the primary functions of Catholic teaching on world order has been to point the way toward a more integrated international system."

Isn't this something?

They are part of a vanguard by ushering in this one-world religious and political system and this is precisely what the Bible declared would come to pass in the final days.

But how do we know we are really in the end times?

Thousands of years ago certain events were predicted, such as the union of seemingly opposing organizations to bring about a one-world political and religious system. Now we are finding all of these religious groups — which were once fighting one another — coming together harmoniously.

The evidence is clear

We have witnessed two religious systems propagating a systematic plan on how they will implement this new world order. It is not going to be a trans-national system with independent citizenships, but a global society with a global citizenship.

But how is this going to come about when you have so many different opinions? It is going to be easy, I assure you, because it is a primary function of these organizations.

It is high on their agenda to bring about this long-desired plan of Lucifer.

The objections which were always raised when prophetic teachers would present these prophetic projections have been erased for the most part. Many of the outward barriers that seemed to distance the various religious groups from one another are now being dismantled in the name of unity. However, the unity among the Adepts within these organizations has always been there.

Indeed, as 2 Thessalonians 2:7 tells us, "For the mystery of iniquity doth already work."

 *Personal Testimonies*

What do people who have left these groups have to say?

Does anyone else — anyone other than me — see the dangers hidden in seemingly benign, pseudo-Christian organizations?

Or am I guilty of Christian paranoia?

No.

In a few pages, we will look at some of the testimonies of good people formerly snared — but now delivered by the grace of our Lord.

In traveling to various parts of the world as a minister, I meet such people who tell me horrid stories of their involvement with esoteric groups.

In those conversations and in my own personal research, I've noted one word repeatedly mentioned — one term which rises regardless of the cult or occultic practice.

Antichrist Associates

What is the word?

'Initiate.'

Remember, these groups remain alive through constant recruitment of the gullible, the naive and the inexperienced.

Initiate.

The dictionary tells us that an initiate is a person being introduced, indoctrinated or oriented before entering a society, discipline or organization. He is one being educated in the ways of an institution formerly foreign to him.

They're evangelizing just like we are.

It is important that these occultists raise initiates to the mysteries of the coming age to help bring about this one-world political and religious system we've been talking about.

When one realizes Satan has been waiting since the beginning of human time to wrest control of Earth, it becomes evident why there would seem to be so much anxiety among the occultists in taking the quantum leap into darkness.

At the time of this writing, New Agers are asking for hundreds of thousands to pray along with them on the last day of December 1986 that nothing will take place in 1987 to hinder their plans. It has been suggested that the New Agers wanted to establish this new order in 1982, which, of course, did not materialize.

What happens to these recruits?

An esoteric initiation is actually a Luciferic initiation. What takes place when an individual is initiated into an esoteric organization is similar to what takes place when a person becomes a born-again Christian.

This is the horrible part which is the principal reason for making this information available. An esoteric initiation is actually a Luciferic initiation. And what really takes place is similar to the baptism of the Holy Ghost in the born-again Christian. However, because this is satanic, it is referred to as an initiation. Sadly enough, when these people give themselves over to this system, they become possessed by a demonic spirit.

In-filled with an evil presence.

The naive people who innocently believe they are serving the God of heaven in some of the organizations mentioned, can actually become possessed with an occultic spirit or spirits, exactly the same way the born-again Christian becomes possessed by the Spirit of the Lord Jesus Christ when that person places their trust in Him.

How to renounce Satan

One of the first things people ask me after presenting a lecture on this subject is, "How can I break away from this after having participated in many of the rituals?"

The answer to this is surprisingly simple.

If you have ever taken part in any of these initiations, it is extremely important that you actually come to God, and ask the Lord Jesus Christ to forgive you of your involvement once you discover the satanic connection.

It is important that you renounce your part by confessing it to the Lord.

A simple, sincere prayer such as this: "Blessed Lord Jesus, forgive my ignorance and participation in anything that was not Godly. I renounce any allegiance I have given ignorantly or intelligently and ask that you forgive me and free me from any occult claims on my life or family. I give myself to you, dear Lord Jesus. I believe by the Bible that you died for my sins and rose again from the grave. Come in to my life and take control. I ask this in Your name, dear Jesus, and for your sake."

I have had many friends — including preachers, deacons and godly men and women — who joined Freemasonry, the Eastern Star or other esoteric groups.

Yet, if they have been through the initiations and have taken upon themselves diabolical spirits, they must renounce that evil.

Having said the above prayer from the heart, we can rest with the assurance of God's Word that if we confess our sins, God is **faithful** and just to forgive us and to cleanse us from **all** unrighteousness — according to I John 1:9.

A white witch's testimony

While I was in South Africa recently I heard the peculiar testimony of a young lady who considered herself to be a white witch. She had participated in various New Age organizations and had taken part in many different initiation rituals. She testified that when she took part in the first initiation, a warm sensation overcame her. She believes it was probably at this time that she experienced her Luciferic initiation.

That is, at this time, she received a demonic spirit of the occult — and became possessed of this Luciferic spirit.

Not unlike Christian in-filling

For born-again believers, there is just one baptism by the Holy Spirit. However, there are many times the Spirit blesses us with peace and joy and strength.

Unfortunately, the opposite can happen in the occult world. When you are initiated the first time, you become demon-possessed. But over a period of time you can take on many demons.

This young girl actually believed she was serving God in a good way. She said to me, "John, I believed and I knew that I was a white witch."

She said she could use mind control on people and that she had many talents or Luciferic gifts.

All the while she believed she was doing good deeds.

As a white witch, she believed she was using her "white magic" to function for God.

A black witch recognizes she uses her black magic for Satan — but not white witches.

The life of this young woman was turned around in Port Elizabeth, South Africa where one of her husband's co-workers witnessed to him. She was of Irish descent, but was born in Kenya. Her husband, born Jewish, began sharing with her his co-worker's testimony.

He brought home literature, which included American author Constance E. Cumbey's book, *The Hidden Dangers Of The Rainbow.*

Her first response was an interesting one. She said to herself, "Well, I'm going to read this book thoroughly, but I'm going to come back to him and show him his fallacy."

After all, she noted, New Agers pride themselves in being open-minded.

I believe that it is this characteristic that leads many to esoteric groups and practices as they open themselves to any enticing doctrine that wanders in from the swamp — particularly when they are not being given any truth or life in the deadness and non-commitment of traditional denominational churches.

They are easy prey for the adversary. They often are searching for something different because they see hypocrisy and lifelessness in Christian churches claiming to have answers and truth. In their rejection of the dead, powerless, unloving God taught in liberal churches, they look elsewhere. Like everyone, they must fulfill the desire that God has created within us to worship the Creator, our Savior Who offers us eternal and abundant life.

But her search landed her in the middle of this New Age initiation.

She received special powers.

A glowing force came over her body, she said.

However, she noted, after a while in the organization, she began developing thoughts of suicide.

Eventually the immorality so prevalent in the group began to trouble her, and she realized it really wasn't what she thought it was going to be.

She really wasn't "one with the universe," and there wasn't just one force working in and through all people.

The information given to her husband by his co-worker arrived just at the right time. She had been contemplating suicide and had withdrawn from the local occultic groups with which she had been meeting.

The questions raised by her husband's friend's tracts and conversation only served to confirm her doubts.

She knew something was very wrong.

As she read *Hidden Dangers of the Rainbow,* she was increasingly impressed by the research and knowledge of the author.

However, she could not bring herself to believe a statement by the author that David Spangler of the Findhorn Foundation was calling for a Luciferic initiation of all New Agers.

Up until this point, she had truly believed that she was a good witch — one that was serving in the best interests of God.

A good witch.

However, her childhood instruction in matters of God served to throw constant doubt into her mind.

She proclaimed one thing aloud, but increasingly, she believed quite another.

As a girl, she had been taught that Lucifer was the devil.

Yet, her friends were being taught to swear allegiance to him.

How could this be?

God and the devil are foes, she knew.

Was she on God's side ...

Or had she been deceived?

She decided to attend a meeting given by representatives of the Findhorn Foundation and ask the lecturers point-blank whether they venerated Satan.

Had she been deceived?

After asking several questions brought out by *Hidden Dangers of the Rainbow*, she came to the crucial question which been plaguing her.

She smiled and, in a seemingly joking manner, asked "Can you believe that David Spangler is actually calling for a Luciferic initiation of all New Agers?"

To her horror, the lecturer looked at her and chastized her:

"Lucifer," the lecturer said, quite calmly, "is our friend."

It was this bold declaration that

revealed to her the evil behind her "white" witchcraft — to the unmistakably hellish force behind all that she had been involved in.

She was horrified ... even terrified.

Soon thereafter she turned her heart and soul over to God, renounced her witchcraft and accepted the salvation of Jesus.

Still, it seemed she was oppressed by demonic spirits.

So she had to go through an exorcism of sorts — a deliverance session freeing her from the demons she had received from the initiations in which she had participated.

Perhaps you were a Mormon.

I really don't want to scare readers. Perhaps you were a Mormon or a Freemason, and you've taken part in these initiations.

Perhaps you were in the Eastern Star, the ladies' auxiliary of the Masons.

Many reading this book may be concerned if they have taken part in a ritualistic initiation of a secret organization.

Depending on the motive or attitude you may have had when you went through these rites, you may or may not have allowed yourself to be infested with demonic spirits.

If you exercised any faith or trust in the occultic leaders or in the dark forces they represented, the chances are very good that you received an occultic spirit.

An evil infestation in your being

Such esoteric organizations start an initiate at the very bottom of the ladder and bring him up slowly to test his obedience.

After a certain point, however, the seething energies of Lucifer are right in the palms of your hands.

How much of his power you have depends how much of yourself you have given over to him with each step up the ladder.

The same principle applies to the occult world, the esoteric world, as applies to Biblical Christianity.

Sometimes nothing much happens.

There are many people who come forward in churches all the time, and they go to the altar and kneel down with the pastor. He leads them in prayer and they simply repeat his words before standing up and walking up the aisle — as lost as when they first approached him. Why is this?

Because they have to believe in their own hearts, and they are doing nothing by simply repeating someone else's words.

They have to give themselves to God.

The Bible is clear on this point: "No one can unto the Son unless the Father draw him."

You have to believe by faith, having heard the Word of God, having been moved by the Spirit of God and having been convicted of your sins by the Holy Ghost.

When this takes place, you yield to the person of the Lord Jesus Christ, and at that moment you are baptized in the Holy Spirit.

You receive the Spirit of Christ, and He takes up residence within you.

But if you merely utter words, you really have received nothing.

Fortunately, many of the people in these organizations — such as the Freemasons — belong to such groups simply for the material or economic benefits. Often they merely repeat words and so they never have been possessed by a demonic spirit.

Antichrist Associates

If this is the case, you are still free, and you are not as much in bondage as are those who actually give themselves over to the Luciferic spirit.

Evil charismatic churches

A neighbor and good friend of mine recently told me about an experience he had while involved in mediation and prayer.

This man was a Mason as well as a Bible student at a charismatic Bible school.

He said he was taught the very same principles in this Bible institute as he had through the Masons in learning to enter the spiritual world.

He told me how he was instructed to "prime the pump," so to speak, by continuously repeating words until they became garbles or when the spirit took over.

This is precisely how the occultists experience an initiation.

Nowhere does the Bible tell us that we need to give the Holy Spirit help to get started in His work in our lives.

He said he would feel a warm energy — known in the occult, as the creative fire — climb up his spinal cord and through his throat, causing what he thought was Biblical tongues (they are called *mantras* in the occult) and he would begin "speaking in tongues."

To my dismay,

I have discovered that hundreds of thousands believe in this same thing.

I personally have never experienced it — for which I am glad.

I have been to a lot of churches where it was practiced.

I have trembled in concern at their ecstatic utterances.

It's just not right.

As my ministry has taken me across the world, I have been able to preach in many churches where this evil is rife.

Several of these churches I have been instructed to raise my hands and say, "Amen." Like the other members of the body, I would do so.

Amen and amen?

Then the pastor would say, "Well, say it over and over and over again. That's how you get to speak in tongues."

And so, in my naiveté, I would say,

"Amen, amen, amen, amen, amen." Well, God protected me, I guess, because He knew that I was sincere but foolish.

I never gave myself over to this.

But as I said it over and over my words became garbled, and then I was asked to say, "Hallelujah" over and over, and again my words became garbled.

Then people instructed me that I was speaking in tongues.

I knew I wasn't, however.

I have seen hundreds of friends go through this process and some were so naive that they walked out of church believing they did speak in tongues.

Some actually went into a trance while doing this, and I believe that what they were really experiencing was a Hindu-like trance.

Nowhere in the Word of God will you find one instance where tongues was ever spoken by merely repeating words over and over and over.

Some church leaders wrongly believe you must "prime the pump" so to speak, by helping out the Holy Spirit. However, the Bible clearly states in Philippians 2:13 that:

"It is God who works in you, both to will and to do of His good pleasure."

Instructions to prime the pump actually originate in the esoteric world.

This is how Satan deceives these individuals into thinking that it is of God when all the time they can become possessed by a demon this way, if they give themselves over to it.

Fortunately —

Most people never become possessed this way. Instead, they have just repeated the words and walked away ignorant. My neighbor and friend who was the Freemason did give himself over to the experience, though he later renounced it and God set him free.

Thus it is with thousands.

They do not speak in tongues.

They merely babble.

But some actually awaken their "psychic centers" or *kundalini* — the serpent power, as it is referred to in other occultic movements. They move into an altered state of consciousness giving the executive control of their faculties over to a medium.

This is the experience my neighbor had.

He lost control.

This is not of God.

No. There seems to be a total lack on the part of such believers to "try the spirits to see if they are of God," as John instructed if we are to defend ourselves against modern Gnostics.

I believe these people are wrong when they instruct others to prime the pump.

The Bible reveals to us that God is the one who is working in us and that He will accomplish **both:**

- the willing and
- the doing —

of his good pleasure.

No suggestion is given at all to priming the pump. The same instruction is given in I Corinthians 12:11:

But all these worketh that one and the self-same Spirit, dividing to every man severally as he will.

Clearly, our will does not ever into

the dispensing of the gifts of the Spirit. He will dispense His gifts to each individual *as He wills.*

My neighbor has since renounced his involvement in these charismatic practices.

God has set him free.

Praise be the Lord.

7

The Serpent Power

Where did all this begin?

Long, long ago.

Satan's deception of man began in the Garden of Eden when the serpent lied to Eve about the power of the forbidden fruit.

Genesis 3:4-5 reads:

"And the serpent said unto the woman, Ye shall not surely die: For God doth know that in the day ye eat thereof, then your eyes shall be opened, and ye shall be as gods, knowing good and evil.

In very clear language, the Bible tells us it was the serpent who beguiled Eve by telling her she would not die if she partook of the forbidden fruit — even though God had instructed her and Adam that they would.

However, there are some people

who do not look at Satan as the wicked, awful devil he is.

The image of the serpent and of snakes in general have always caused people to shiver. Instead they look at him from a different, perverted perspective.

According to the June 15, 1973 Deseret News, Mormon leader Brigham Young stated in a service at the Mormon Tabernacle in Salt Lake City:

The devil told the truth. I do not blame Mother Eve. I would not have had her miss eating the forbidden fruit for anything in the world. They must pass through the same ordeals as the gods, that they may know good from evil.

What?

This is an astonishing statement from a religious leader whose followers make a claim that they believe in the Bible — and considering the fact that the Word of God clearly identifies Satan as a wicked individual who rebelled against God and wanted to exalt his own throne against that of the Creator.

As if the account of Man's Fall in the first chapters of Genesis is not clear enough, look at II Corinthians 11:3 —

But I fear, lest by any means, as the serpent beguiled Eve through his subtilty, so your minds should be corrupted from the simplicity that is in Christ.

This is not biblical.

There is not the slightest suggestion from God's Word that the devil told the truth. This is another example of what takes place when religions blend seeming Biblical teachings with occultic teachings.

Bible doctrines become perverted and the many disciples who come in to these organizations are the ones who suffer and possibly go on to a lost eternity.

This modern Gnosticism has been making inroads into historical Christianity for two thousand years now — and continues to experience great success. *The Message of the Stars*, a book giving an esoteric exposition of natal and medical astrology, gives us an insight into some of the thinking of gnostics. On page 724-725, we read:

There was a time, even as late as

that of Greece, when religion, art and science were taught unitedly in the Mystery Temples ... Religion held sole sway in the so-called "dark ages" ... It was a detriment to the world when religion shackled science ... Such a state cannot continue ... Therefore steps were taken to spiritualize science and make religion scientific. (Science simple means knowledge, to know) ... In the 13th Century, a high spiritual teacher, having the symbolic name Christian Rosenkreutz, appeared in Europe to commence that work.

He founded the mystical Order of Rosicrucians with the object of throwing occult light upon the misunderstood Christian religion and to explain the mystery of life and being from the scientific standpoint in harmony with religion.

What a clear illustration of "blending" — of satanic perversion of the Church's truths.

The intent:

To bring religion and science together, water down Christianity, throw in a little Hinduism, Druidism, ancient astrology and nature worship, then package it all together with a dose of mysticism.

It certainly *looks* religious. But the purpose was to bring the occult into Christianity — to explain the mysteries of life from an esoteric perspective.

This is gnosticism.

It is the mixing of certain Christian traditions with esoteric beliefs. But it results in perversion of the Biblical message. The occult is dished up and served on a platter to those attending esoteric functions. Sometimes these evil events are taking place in our church, involving innocent men and women who participate, believing they are serving God.

This work of Satan is growing through what is known today as the New Age movement.

This is nothing new, however.

It is nothing more than the old lie of the Garden that is gaining greater acceptance through false esoteric teachings.

This same book, *The Message of the Stars,* on pages 20-21 gives us added insight into other views on the serpent:

In looking up the word "serpent" in the Bible, we shall find that there are about seven words that have been thus translated ...

The *Message of the Stars* asserts that one of the words was taken from Egypt and is *Naja.*

In ancient Egypt, according to this occultic text, the ruler wore a headdress decorated with a double serpent, which was called the Uraeus Naja. It was said to be an emblem of cosmic wisdom and gave the appearance of coming out of the forehead.

Serpent and mind, king and priest.

This symbolized the dual role of king and priest. It is said that in India, the guardians of these mystic teachings are called *Nagas* or serpents.

When I shared this information in South Africa, there were several people from India in attendence. One who was employed at the zoo came to me and told me that the cobra snake had *naga* inscribed across what he indicated to me would be the neck or throat.

The *Message of the Stars* goes on to give a common belief between

King Tut — *note the double serpent decorating the headdress*

them and Masonry on pages 23-24:

> *... Every Freemason knows that the brethren of that order are called "Sons of the Widow." ... a widow's son or initiate of the old serpent school ...*

each had within, the ancient serpent wisdom. But a new religion was being inaugurated, and it was necessary to raise the ancient initiates to the mysteries of the coming age.

Test the spirits.

This is one area believers must test the spirits to determine whether the teachings are in harmony with the Word of God found in the Bible.

Let us take a bit of print space here to contract the manner in which the Bible portrays the serpent. We have already shown passages which reveal the snake as beguiling Eve.

In Matthew 23:27 and 33, Jesus said:

Woe unto you, scribes and Pharisees, hypocrites! for ye are like unto whited sepulchers, which indeed appear beautiful outward, but are within full of dead men's bones, and of all uncleanness ... Ye serpents, ye generation of vipers, how can you escape the damnation of hell?

There is not one word of commendation given whenever the term serpent is given to any one individual. It is always given within the context of condemnation.

A text taken out of context which is used by the mystics, however, to commend its use is when Jesus instructed His disciples to be "wise as serpents."

He said this not to commend the serpent, but because of the subtlety and craftiness associated with it.

Never a compliment.

Whenever the Word of God identifies people as serpents or vipers, it is because they are under condemnation and their intent is evil.

But we recognize, on the other hand, that the esoteric new age groups throughout the world today actually call themselves serpents and do so proudly.

The Masons even have this one particular order they call the "sons of the widow," who are nothing more than serpent initiates.

Filled with an evil spirit

These initiates actually are individuals who have given themselves over to a Luciferic spirit. Satan's spirit has come and taken up residence within them just as the Spirit of the living Christ comes and takes up residence in every born-again child of God.

Antichrist Associates

It is extremely important to understand that going through an esoteric initiation is something to be dreaded and feared because you can become demon possessed.

According to page 48 of Manly P. Hall's *The Lost Keys Of Freemasonry:*

Beware:

"When the Mason has learned the mystery of his craft, at that time the seething energies of Lucifer are in his hands, and before he may step onwards and upward, he must prove his ability to properly apply this energy."

Recipients of Satanic power

Notice here that these esoteric organizations take upon themselves these Luciferic initiations and then proudly proclaim to the world that they have this seething energy of Lucifer's in their hands.

This reveals just how far this delusion has come, when people can proclaim this twisted, black event with pride.

We find another use of the serpent in a book by Arthur Avalon entitled, *The Serpent Power, the Secrets of Tantric and Shaktic Yoga.*

On the back cover, the author says:
Who is Kundalini, the Serpent Power? ... She is the mysterious power that resides in the human body and can be awakened through suitable techniques: special meditations and yogic practices of a particularly powerful nature.

It is taught that this power can be awakened through special meditations and yogic practices.

A yogi simply means one who is a "seeker of light."

A guru is known as one who is a "dispeller of light."

Darkness amid light.

So this power, this mysterious power that resides in the human body can be awakened through suitable techniques.

One who practices yoga is seeking the light, which actually is Lucifer himself.

"She is the goddess, the ultimate heart of many areas of eastern religion, not only of Hinduism."

There are hundreds and thousands of Christian churches across

Antichrist Associates

America today that actually are having — under the guise of exercise — yoga classes and special meditations. But our research shows clearly these meditations are designed for one specific purpose: to awaken the serpent power.

Ephesians 2:2 states:

"Wherein in time past you walked according to the course of this world, according to the prince of the power of the air, the spirit that now works in the children of disobedience."

The apostle Paul was saying that once a person disobeys God and he gives himself over to these diabolical practices, Lucifer will possess this person.

It is tragic.

But it is taking place.

One cannot participate in any of these meditations and special yogic practices under the guise of relaxation or exercise and not be affected in some spiritual sense.

These practices are first and foremost religious-spiritual.

The apostle Paul refers to this power that would come upon people when they would enter a state of disobedience toward God.

And it is not of God.

Indeed, yoga is being practiced by various organizations, by various movements and groups under different names — and ever more commonly in churches where members gather during the week to meditate, relax and sit in yoga positions.

But Satan has one purpose in mind when he brings such perversion into the church: to draw the believer into a deeper spiritual relationship with himself and not God.

According to the Rosicrucians' book, *The Message Of the Stars:*

"...the creative fire is drawn upwards through the serpentine spinal cord. Then it vibrates the pituitary gland, connecting the ego — the inner you — with the invisible powers. The creative cosmic fire is drawn upward, though the head, to serve a spiritual end."

Yes, the battle for the mind is perfectly clear.

This is the ultimate design behind the special meditations of all forms of yoga. It is to place you in contact with the cosmic entities placing the executive control of your mind under their control.

It is not merely that of exercise or meditation.

The design behind this is spiritual.

It is a religious practice, and it places you in communication with other spirits.

This is how Satan — the wicked serpent as defined by the Bible — wants to gain control of your mind.

Beware.

 The Battle for Mind Control

How can we fight back?

Are we powerless against Lucifer's assault?

No. We're conqerers.

The Bible stresses that we are not to quake in fear of the deceiver.

His primary tools are fear and lies.

Jesus has all power over him.

The battle has already been fought.

And we have won.

But we cannot stress enough the need for the Christian to train himself to be perceptive.

We must be more fervent in our prayer life and commitment to the Lord Jesus Christ. The born-again believer has to be more perceptive of the enemy's lies and perversions today than ever before.

We have to pray more fervently than ever to God, to the Lord Jesus

Christ and the Holy Spirit, whom the Father sent to instruct us and lead us into all truth.

There are many false teachers out there, and Satan has released them with a renewed vengeance upon this world.

Because his time is short, he is intensifying his efforts to confuse seekers of truth today.

But one of the greatest tragedies of his perversion of the Gospel and his infiltration of the Church is that many Christian pastors and teachers are naively teaching Gnosticism in their churches and bringing people to a position where they can become demon possessed.

Tempting falsehoods.

The flair for something new and exciting has added to the suscept-ibility of the pastors of exciting and growing churches on the rise.

Many Christians, thinking they are coming to the Holy Spirit, are actually becoming possessed though esoteric practices that have invaded the church of Jesus Christ today.

There exists, for example, a special chanting ritual performed in Mormon temples which is straight from the occult. Mormons actually promote this chant saying, "We desire all to receive it, and all will arise."

Tragically,

They haven't a clue what they are going to receive.

According to the Mormon passage describing the ritual:

"Then each of them will make the sign of the second token of the Melchizedek priesthood. They will perform the patriarchal grip, or the sure sign of the nail by raising both hands above the head and by lowering their hands to the side ...."

As they continue through this ritual, they utter the following chant:

Pay Lay Ale.
Pay Lay Ale.
Pay Lay Ale.

This is repeated as they raise and lower their hands, but they do not have the slightest idea of the meaning of the chant.

Translated from the Hebrew, this expression actually means, "O wonderful Lucifer."

They think they are coming closer to the Lord Jesus Christ, but actually they are praising Satan.

Shocking?
Yes.

And when they say, "We desire all to receive it," they actually are extending an invitation and instruction on how to receive the Luciferic initiation, the Satanic ritual which pervades all of these esoteric organizations.

The initiates can innocently think they are coming to serve the Lord Jesus Christ, but actually they are leaving demon possessed.

In His earthly teachings, Christ said:
"But when you pray use not vain repetitions as the heathen do." (Matthew 6:7)

And so these vain repetitions and chants, the repetitions of prayer over and over again — even of words you understand — are not to be used. This action is intended for the single purpose of arousing that serpentine spinal cord, the creative fire. It actually is a demon love call.

All our research on Satan's

esoteric organizations points to one significant fact: There is a fierce battle going on today for your mind. God wants to control your mind, but so does Satan.

Philippians 2:5 states:

"Let this mind be in you which was also in Christ Jesus."

God wants this mind that was in Jesus to be in you. That is the clear Word of God. The Father wants you to give yourself over to the study of the Bible so that you can be equipped to fight these demonic powers when they come against you.

God wants this mind to be in you that was in our Lord Jesus, through the scriptures, the Word of God. The Word is what equips you for the battle as a good soldier of the Savior.

Mind control?

Another example of this battle over control of our minds is found in *The Silva Mind Control Method: The Revolutionary Program by the Founder of the World's Most Famous Mind Control Course* by Jose Silva.

But who is going to be in control of your mind if you follow this method? The answer becomes tragically clear as you read through the book.

I hope you never experience the meditation promoted by this method because you would be seeking the serpent power we discussed in the last chapter.

You'd be playing into Satan's hand.

Through this book we learn there is more than one way to stir up this power. The author states in the fourth chapter, entitled *Dynamic Meditation:*

*The passive meditation you have just read about (and I hope are about to experience) can be accomplished in other ways. Instead of concentrating on a visual image, you can concentrate on a sound such as **om** or **one** or **amen,** uttered aloud or mentally or the feeling of your breathing.*

Om is a term used by many esoteric organizations throughout the world. According to those who know, it is full of power.

Once you use that term in a chant, you will surely get a quick response from the occult world.

The same is true if you use "amen."

It will get the quick attention of certain counselors, entities or spirit guides as these spirits are also referred to.

According to this book, you can focus on an energy point, the beat of a drum, a dance, a chant — even religious words.

The warning of Jesus to his followers was to not say repetitious prayers "as the heathen do." This was because this repetition was designed by a Luciferic conspiracy to awaken the serpent power.

Use of chants in churches

According to the Rosicrucian cathechism, *The Master Monograph:*

In many of the ancient religious ceremonies, chants in either Latin or Hebrew are used.

And in both cases, the vowel sounds are identical and some of them are drawn out, in long sounds, that even seem weird to persons who do not understand.

Tragically, our research revealed that many Christian churches throughout the world also promote chants, and many of these chants date back to the earliest esoteric movements.

This is another example of Gnosticism, the blending of the occult with Biblical Christianity, and this is why Christians are given the warning, "Beware, lest any man deceive you by any means."

The Hindu "Om"

According to page 33 of a book about Earth's major religious movements, *The World's Great Religions*, published by *Time* magazine, the word *om* is the most sacred single syllable in Hinduism. They teach that whosoever knows this syllable obtains all that he desires. This word is considered one of Hinduism's divine principles.

Hindus believe that the word 'om' is one key to receiving the power of immortality.

According to this book, the word is on the lips of devout Hindus from the cradle to the grave, and it refers to a Hindu god.

Yet this term is being used as well by many esoteric groups throughout the world — as well as a growing number of "therapists," holistic healers, psychologists, psychiatrists, positive-thinking proponents and supposed mental health counselors. It is innocently being used in many Christian churches as well.

How tragic!

It would be wonderful if people everywhere could understand the dangers of this because they are being bombarded with this esoteric garbage constantly.

Especially in the business world, people are exposed to positive mental attitude courses or meditation sessions which are nothing more than Luciferic teachings. Through these teachings Satan hopes to gain control of their minds, that they might usher in this one-world conspiracy.

It shows up in Freemasonry, too.

Page 82 of the book *Morals and Dogma of Freemasonry* declares:

Buddha is declared to comprehend in his own person the essence of the Hindu Trimurti; and hence the triliteral monosyllable om or aum is applied to him as being essentially the same as Brahma-Vishnu-Siva.

The book goes on to say that *om* is

also represented by the ancient esoteric symbol of life of the early Egyptians.

This Hindu monosyllable is also represented by the mystic character Y which can be found displayed above the doors of the Church of the Holy Sepulcher in Jerusalem.

What is illustrated in most of these esoteric symbols is a spiritual sexual union, the bringing together of the opposites.

What you actually see is that Satan desires to have spiritual intercourse with people in this world. That is what is taking place when people undergo a Luciferic initiation.

Cross and rose, yin and yang

This is what is represented in the symbol of the triangle and in the Rosicrucian cross and rose, the Oriental *yin* and *yang* and in the compass and square of the Masonic Lodge.

A spiritual intercourse with Earth.

That's what Lucifer and his demons desire to have with the peoples and nations of the world.

And this is what happens when one gives up one's mind to demonic influence.

Spiritual rape.

God's Word declared thousands of years ago that Satan's power would become stronger in the end times. When we see it coming about, we ought to become excited — because it proves that God's Word is true.

It is being fulfilled, however.

It's being fulfilled right before our very eyes, through the members of these esoteric organizations.

This fulfillment of prophecy ought to be used by all students of the Bible to assure the weak that God is indeed in control of things.

As we cited earlier from *The Silva Mind Control Method,* it is suggested that "all of these methods and some combination of them will bring you to a calm, meditative level of mind. This is contrasted with the manner in which the believer is comforted by 'his' God."

Such blasphemy!

And so bold.

Satan is aware of what is happening, and he knows his time is short. He doesn't want to spend eternity by himself or with just a few. He wants to take with him as many as he can. But I don't want you to spend your time with him. I want you to spend eternity with the Lord Jesus Christ in heaven.

This is God's desire as well.

So beware!

Esoteric organizations are insidious.

They trick us into thinking "terrible" is "wonderful."

And the damage can be terrible.

Just look at the condition of children's Saturday morning cartoons. They virtually comprise a textbook on demonology.

Youngsters learn about incantations, crystal balls, wise wizards, "good magic" and mind power. Look at the discount store toys that spin off from these cartoons. The evil opponents are available in doll form for our youngsters to take into their rooms.

They, too, can play at defeating the magic-wielding good guys — but by using admittedly evil sorcery against his supposedly good powers.

Hypnosis and self-hypnosis are offered everywhere, too, it seems. I see these techniques as examples of making spiritual contact with Lucifer.

Esoteric group leaders often emphasize frequent practice of meditation and self-hypnosis so the individual can become very skilled in his efforts.

Meanwhile, in many Christian churches today people walk in the door lost and after the limp-wristed sermon, they leave lost, confused and willing to look elsewhere for answers.

Although they have heard the gospel of the grace of God and they have heard the plan of salvation, their hearts have been unchanged. This is tragic because now more than ever it is important to fight off the spirit of Satan and take on the full armour of God.

It's all a mighty conspiracy.

Cosmic Christianity has permeated the entire world. All of these esoteric religions will gather together easily when the final reign of the Antichrist begins. Once the rapture takes place, however, all the born-again Christians will be lifted up out of this world. Left behind will be the false religion of Satan and the leaders and members of these esoteric organizations.

Yes, this cosmic consciousness has pervaded the entire world.

Antichrist Associates

When the people of God leave at the last trumpet sound, the Antichrist will have his day.

He will govern this earth for a seven-year period until Christ Jesus returns to set up His reign for 1,000 years on earth.

In closing —

We would like to conclude this chapter with a passage from II Peter 3:11-13:

Seeing then that all these things shall be dissolved, what manner of persons ought ye to be in all holy conversation and godliness, looking for and hasting unto the coming of the day of God, wherein the heavens being on fire shall be dissolved, and the elements shall melt with fervent heat? Nevertheless, we, according to his promise, look for new heavens and a new earth, wherein dwelleth righteousness.

Mysticism
Within Christian
Organizations

Whenever it is suggested that some form of false teaching is being propagated by a denomination, a church or a certain pastor, evangelist or Christian leader, most Christians react with astonishment and disbelief.

Accusers are treated as the accused.

The accuser is counseled not to bring his charges public, because it will hurt the church —

Even if the false teachings and esoteric seduction of the offending pastor is leading thousands straight into the jaws of Hell!

So, what are we to do?

Politely sit back, hinting obliquely that some are misguided, but well-meaning?

No! That's not what the Bible says.

II Corinthians 11: 13-15 states:

Antichrist Associates

> *For such are false apostles, deceitful workers, transforming themselves into the apostles of Christ. And no marvel; for Satan himself is transformed into an angel of light. Therefore it is no great thing if his ministers also be transformed as the ministers of righteousness; whose end shall be according to their works.*

I must expose evil.

And so I will.

When the goal of the Antichrist is understood by Christians, when they can understand through the study of the prophetic Word in the Bible, then they will accept and test the spirits to see if they are of the Lord.

It is easily understood that any effort to establish a global government is certainly not a movement that is going to glorify the Lord Jesus Christ.

The goal of the New Age movement is to bring about global unity for the purpose of worshiping the Antichrist when he comes.

We have seen many esoteric symbols so far which link certain international organizations and show they already are working together for global unity.

Besides the triple crown of

godhood, the crossed keys and the Egyptian symbol of life, another parallel among esoteric groups is the veneration of the mother and child.

In the Roman Catholic church, for example, you have the worship of the mother and child — Mary and Jesus. But this is the only Christian church that promotes this teaching, which is prominent in other religions throughout the world.

The Hindus, for example, have a similar practice of the veneration of mother and child. We see the same practice in Egyptian literature as well. All of this is by design, and it shows the link between a seemingly Christian organization and the occult.

I'm sure there are many many lovely Roman Catholic people, who love the Lord Jesus Christ, and love His Bible and are not aware of these similarities between their teachings and those from clearly esoteric organizations.

Church members — like participants in various esoteric organizations — are deliberately misled by church leaders. They are given false ideas, and false explanations. False teachings of what these things represent, all the while, leading them down a path that perhaps for many will lead to destruction.

Catholics and the Rosicrucians

By reviewing the official publications of the Rosicrucian Society, the Ancient and Mystical Order of the Rosae Crucis, we discover an interesting parallel between that esoteric organization and the Roman Catholic Church.

It is in the form of an astonishing illustration that could possibly be another form of symbolic communication between the Adepts of these religious organizations.

Is it really of the cross?

The booklet entitled *The Rosicrucian Initiation* has a special illustration which caught my attention. The illustration is called Illustration No. 3 on a chart with other illustrations and is to illustrate how the official "Sign of the Cross" is made.

Having been a member of the Roman Catholic religion, I am more than a little familiar with the details of this special sign.

It is a gesture made by Catholics when they enter their church. It is made by touching the forehead, then the center of the breastbone, then both shoulders.

But in making the sign of the cross, Catholics also are creating the symbol of a triangle, which is symbolic of the serpent spirit or Satan.

Triangle power.

Now I'm sure that most Roman Catholics are not aware of this.

They don't think of the sign of the cross as the serpent, as do the Rosicrucians, the Egyptians and other occult organizations.

Many Catholics love Jesus Christ.

But like people in other religious organizations and groups, they are just lead astray and deceived.

This is why the Bible frequently exhorts the born-again believer, "Let no man deceive you by any means."

But we are living in times when Satan is intensifying his efforts to such a degree that very little faith is to be found anywhere throughout the world today.

And this is precisely how the Word of God said it would be.

You might be surprised to learn that the Sign of the Cross of the

Roman Catholic Church is also sacred to the Rosicrucians. In their sacred texts, illustrations of the pattern indicate that it, indeed, is a triangle — not a cross.

In their books, at the point that the two lines "cross," you see a rose, which illustrates the flowering or fruition of the union.

Sexual gods.

According to Tantric belief, an illustration is made of a Tibetan bronze statue of the god Hevajra with his goddess Shakti in a sexual union. According to Tantric belief, such divine union keeps the universe in perfect balance. The cult's sexual rituals aim to bring the cultists in resonance with the divine equilibrium. It is bizarre how all of this different symbology is tied together among the different religious movements.

Occult classes taught in churches

Mainline Protestant churches are also taking part in allowing occult practices to come into their sanctuaries, seminars and Sunday schools.

We found that many so-called

Christian churches were willing to open their doors to certain classes which are clearly of the occult.

For instance, one Methodist church in Tulsa recently offered a "Meditation and Journaling" workshop. According to their brochure, "Participants will use scripture, meditation, guided imagery and writing to take themselves on a journey through seven dimensions of the spirit life."

A class schedule from the Tulsa Learning Community shows several other churches in the city were willing to open their doors to esoteric classes as well. One class on yoga meditation was being held at a Presbyterian church. Another class, on handwriting analysis, is being held at a Christian church.

An evil deluge of perversion

And you find all of these esoteric teachings just flooding into the church today. Sadly, there are many innocent people coming to these organizations thinking they are going to be fed the Word of God. But all the while they are being led down this great chasm where they are being deceived.

A class on numerology was being

held at another Presbyterian church. This is clearly an esoteric science, and yet it is being taught in a church in Tulsa.

How can this be?

II Corinthians 11: 3-4 clearly says:

> *But I fear, lest by any means, as the serpent beguiled Eve through his subtlety, so your minds should be corrupted from the simplicity that is in Christ. For he that comes preaches another Jesus, whom we have not preached, or if you receive another spirit, which you have not received, or another gospel which you have not accepted, you might well bear with them.*

Diluted, perverted Gospel

Unfortunately, too many Christian churches are just allowing their teachings of historic Christianity to be diluted and perverted so that very few people can experience the forgiveness of personal sins through the Lord Jesus Christ today.

That, of course, is the true purpose of Bible-oriented Christian churches. But the delusion goes on and on.

In his book entitled, *The Potential Principle*, Edwin Louis Cole writes: "One of the most important things you can do in life is create an image."

Now according to the Bible, the second commandment is, "Thou shalt not make unto yourselves any graven images." Yet here is this man who states that one of the most important things you can do is create an image.

But even worse, this author cites Psalms 115: 4-8 to back up his beliefs:

"Their idols (or images) are silver and gold, the world of men's hands. They have mouths, but they speak not; eyes have they, but they see not; They have ears, but they hear not; noses have they, but they smell not; They have hands, but they handle not; feet have they, but they walk not; neither speak they through their throat. They that make them are like unto them. So is everyone that trusteth in them."

This is so tragic, and yet I see hundreds and thousands of people who are being fed books and classes about this. I have presented my study in a few churches across the United States, and several people have come up to me afterwards and said, "John,

Antichrist Associates

I've presented material like positive imaging in my church. What is wrong with it?"

Then I explain more about the esoteric aspects of the books and classes and they say, "Oh my goodness, how could I have allowed this to happen?" I exhort all readers: "Let no man deceive you by any means." The tactics of the luciferians throughout the world are being expanded, and they are broadening their efforts that they might establish this global unity, this new age that the Bible predicted would happen. We don't want you to be caught up in that vortex.

Rosicrucian seal at "Christian" school

One official seal of the Ancient and Mystical Order Of The Rosae Crucis depicts two pyramids. One is upside down and the other upright. However, this design — which usually represents this occult — also is used prevalently in the architecture and on the seal of Oral Roberts University in Tulsa, Oklahoma. A similar symbol is found on the letterhead of the City of Faith Medical and Research Center.

You must realize that those of the esoteric world communicate by using symbols. Now this doesn't necessarily mean the people at Oral Roberts University are part of the occult. But when I see a Christian organization using a symbol that is ordinarily used to represent the occult, then a little alarm goes off that tells me to examine their teachings in light of Scripture.

Beware!

When you see these symbols in Christian circles, then that ought to serve as a warning to you to stop and check the organization and its teaching.

10

Symbols:
Telltale Signs of Quiet Infiltration

Symbols tell a great deal.

What does this mean?

Most people do not place such significance on symbols or their use. They would use them simply for design effect.

However, one must also realize that the esoteric community gives extreme importance to the use of symbols. Many in occult organizations place even more importance in communicating through symbols than through the use of words.

But, you may say, can't the triangle also signify the Trinity?

Indeed, isn't that what the people at ORU have in mind?

The symbols used by Oral Roberts University and the City of Faith Medical Center do not declare in themselves that these organizations are occultic or that they are using them to communicate with others in the occult.

Triangles are used by many for the simple purpose of art and design.

But they are not the sole property of those who would symbolize the Father, the Son and the Holy Spirit.

As I have said before, when I see any organization using a symbol I know is used to represent a certain ideal in the occult, an alarm goes off in my head.

Suspicion wells up in my mind.

I step warily around the offensive organization.

I begin looking for the true evil that I know may lurk within.

I tread lightly as I investigate some of the teachings of the organization to see whether, in fact, they also may be mystical and aligned with Satan.

Check their teachings.

They teach young people to speak in tongues as is taught in esoteric groups regarding utterances, tongues. They utter repetitious words to "prime the pump."

They conduct healing seminars,

drawing believers from across the globe to "learn" how to channel God's power through their own prayers.

I am reminded of the Pharisees who looked at Jesus' miracles and wondered if, indeed, this was just proof that He was in league with Satan. I look at the exhortation in God's Word to try the spirits to see if they are of God. And that's exactly what I did with ORU and the City of Faith.

Is their founder, Oral Roberts, a practitioner of orthodox, Bible-believing Christianity?

Is Jesus Lord in his life?

Are his teachings compatible with those of historic Christianity?

First of all, we would like to begin by sharing a comment by Dr. Kurt E. Koch, a noted author and theologian who is recognized as an expert on the occult. We take the following comments from a book he co-authored with Dr. Alfred Lechler, a psychiatrist who is also well acquainted with the esoteric invasion in the lives of people.

The book we will quote from is entitled, *Occult Bondage and Deliverance.* Let's examine pages 52-53 in

Antichrist Associates

this book published by Kregel Publications:

I come now to a painful duty I have put off for many years. However, after a great deal of prayer, I feel I must fulfill the obligation which God has placed on me. In the autumn of 1966, together with about 2,000 other delegates, observers and staff members, I attended the World Congress on Evangelism in Berlin. Among the leaders of the various discussion groups was Oral Roberts, a man who had been publicly greeted by Billy Graham on the platform.

As a fellow delegate, I wrote to the committee, informing them of the fact that the healing ability of Oral Roberts was of a mediumistic rather than a charismatic nature.

The letter caused a lot of anger among those who read it and the next day Billy Graham introduced Oral Roberts a second time to the great audience, putting his arm around his shoulder and addressing him by the name of brother. I have been troubled for some years now by this lack of discernment on the part of Billy Graham and his committee. Previously I have been unprepared to write about *it for fear of damaging their work a work which I personally value, and which I in no wise wish to hinder.*

However, on account of the immense amount of damage which is being caused by Oral Roberts in many areas of the world, I feel unable to remain silent any longer ... To argue that Oral Roberts has founded a university, or has collected millions of dollars for the kingdom of heaven, is no proof that he derived his healing ability from God.

It could just as easily be said that, since Harry Edwards has collected thousands of pounds for his healing ministry and has become the leader of an organization numbering over 2,000 spiritual healers, his powers must be of divine origin, which is patently not true.

Does Jesus appear to men?

In my research I recently reviewed a book entitled *St. Germaine on Alchemy — For the Adept in the Aquarian Age,* which is about a famous American artist of the 1920s and 30s.

With the emphasis on imagery and many Christian leaders claiming occasional and sometimes frequent visible visitations from Jesus, an article on page 259 interested me greatly. It concerns this famed painter, Charles Sindelar.

According to the book:

Jesus Christ appeared to the artist on 22 consecutive mornings at 2 a.m., and the image of the Master would appear throughout the day over both canvas and etching plate, distracting him from his work until he took the advise of a friend to "paint what you have seen."

What is really going on here?

Here is an obvious occultist who had these supposed apparitions of Christ appear to him several times.

The Bible is clear on this point: We are not to make any graven images.

No one knows what Jesus looks like.

The paintings in the book included two images. On the left is Jesus Christ, who the artist refers to as the "ascended master."

On the right is the face of St. Germaine, another ascended master.

Both men are identical in appearance except Jesus has a little longer hair.

The Bible probably commanded us not to make any graven images because we might paint the picture of a demon instead. The artist would be allowing himself to give devotion to a demonic being.

I have heard many people, including preachers, say the person of Jesus appeared to them.

If someone tells you this, do not believe it, because it does not really happen.

Let me repeat that:

If someone tells you this, do not believe it, because it does not really happen.

The command from the Scriptures is clear. We are ordered not to make any graven image or likeness of anything — even if it is from Heaven!

That is absolute.

No likeness of anything, even if it is from heaven.

The aparition could very easily have been an occultic spirit.

It could have been anything!

This could be the reason that the traditional "face of Jesus" draws a great amount of devotion from those who think it to be the likeness of Jesus. Images or idols of any sort are never to be given devotion.

That is a practice totally forbidden by the Bible.

We are to worship God in the spirit and in truth, as the Gospel of John 4:24 so clearly exhorts us to.

Oral's vision of Jesus:

The June 1985 issue of *Charisma* magazine included an article about Oral Roberts.

In describing one hospital experience, he said:

That afternoon, recovering from my surgery, I was praying in my hospital room. Jesus came into my room. He put His hand on me and said, "If you will give, I will give to you." Then I saw an angel in the corner of my room. He said, "Dispatch me."

I didn't know what that meant. He said, "Well, Jesus came into the room and told you what to do, but you can't do it by yourself. You command me to bring in what you need."

I have never read in the Bible where a similar event happened to any apostle, prophet or any man of God.

And in Oral Robert's description of the Lord, there is a lack of reverence given to the Saviour.

It seems more like he is talking about a neighbor or relative or casual friend.

This offends me.

In testing the spirits, I have never read in the Bible where a similar event ever happened.

I know of no apostle, prophet or man of God who ever gave such a testimony.

II Corinthians 5: 7 and 16 says:

"We walk by faith and not by sight ...Though we have known Christ, after the flesh, yet henceforth, know we him no more."

Walk by faith, not by sight!

Thus, if a person tells you he has seen Jesus don't believe it, because the Bible says that the Christian today is to walk by faith, not by sight.

Many have told me they have seen Jesus, and I ask them, "What did He look like?"

What they describe to me is the

exact illustration of the likeness created by this occultist and artist of the 1920s.

By this I can readily detect that they have not seen the Jesus Christ of the Bible.

Consider what the apostle John saw when he saw the glorified Lord Jesus Christ as revealed in Revelation 1: 13-15 and 17:

In the midst of the seven candlesticks one like unto the Son of Man clothed with a garment down to the foot, and girt about the waist with the golden girdle.

His head and His hair were white like wool, as white as snow; and His eyes were as a flame of fire; and His feet like unto fine brass, as if they burned in a furnace; and His voice as the sound of many waters .... And when I saw Him I fell at His feet as dead.

Now here is a man who was familiar with the Lord Jesus Christ and even ministered with Him for at least three years. But when he saw the glorified Jesus, John did not see Christ in the flesh but rather the glorified Jesus Christ.

Tongues — a world-changing power?

Charisma magazine also quoted Oral Roberts as saying,

"I pray in tongues 30 or 40 times a day. That is how I built the City of Faith. This kind of prayer sparks my mind, and I live in that rhythm. This releases great power which will change the world."

Sometimes prayer in tongues can be compared to Hindu chanting.

These chants actually are used to awaken the "psychic center" or draw out the serpent power within.

Nowhere in the Bible will you find any man of God saying that prayer in tongues will change the world. Paul cautions us in I Corinthians 14: 2-19:

For he that speaketh in an unknown tongue speaketh not unto men, but unto God: for no man understandeth him; howbeit in the spirit he speaketh mysteries.

But he that prophesieth speaketh unto men to edification and comfort. He that speaketh in an unknown tongue edifieth himself; but he that prophesieth edifieth the church. I would that ye all spake with tongues, but rather that ye prophesied: for greater is he that prophesieth than he that speaketh with tongues, except he interpret, that the church may receive edifying.

Paul continues:

Now, brethren, if I come unto you speaking with tongues, what shall I profit you, except I shall speak to you either by revelation, or by knowledge, or by prophesying, or by doctrine? And even things without life giving sound, whether pipe or harp, except they give a distinction in the sounds, how shall it be known what is piped or harped? For if the trumpet give an uncertain sound, who shall prepare himself to the battle? So likewise ye, except ye utter by the tongue words easy to be understood, how shall it be known what is spoken? for ye shall speak into the air.

There are, it may be, so many kinds of voices in the world, and none of them is without signification. Therefore if I know not the meaning of the voice, I shall be unto him that speaketh a barbarian, and he that speaketh shall be a barbarian unto me.

So ye, forasmuch as ye are zealous

of spiritual gifts, seek that ye may excel to the edifying of the church.

Wherefore let him that speaketh in an unknown tongue pray that he may interpret. For if I pray in an unknown tongue, my spirit prayeth, but my understanding is unfruitful. What is it then?

I will pray with the spirit, and I will pray with the understanding also: I will sing with the spirit, and I will sing with the understanding also.

Else when thou shalt bless with the spirit, how shall he that occupieth the room of the unlearned say Amen at thy giving of thanks, seeing he understandeth not what thou sayest? For thou verily givest thanks well, but the other is not edified.

And he concludes:

I thank my God, I speak with tongues more than ye all; Yet in the church I had rather speak five words with my understanding, that by my voice I might teach others also, than ten thousand words in an unknown tongue.

The Word of the Lord is clear:

You can read the many books on theology and nowhere will you find testimony like that of Oral Roberts.

Rosicrucian teaching on meditation states:

Most of the breathing and concentration exercises, most of the vowel sounds and vowel exercises are for awakening and enlivening these two small transformers or psychic centers. A certain amount of time is required with each individual before these two become active enough to begin to function properly.

Here you see that all these exercises, including praying in esoteric tongues, are for one purpose and that is awakening the psychic nerve center.

Again, we say:

Test the spirits and you will not be able to find anything in the Bible to suggest such a constant speaking in tongues as Oral Roberts suggests. You will not find a similar comment, either, from any Bible-believing theologian of historical Christianity.

Another simile in the occult world to compare with Oral Roberts' comment about the praying in tongues that releases great power is found in the book *The Serpent Power* by Arthur Avalon, which we quoted earlier.

On the back page, the author says:

> *... the mysterious power that resides in the human body ... can be awakened (or released) through suitable techniques: special meditations and yogic practices of a particularly powerful nature.*

Signs and wonders?

A group of national charismatic leaders met recently in Texas to create an organization called the Charismatic Bible Ministries. According to the March-April 1986 *Abundant Life* magazine, published by Oral Roberts, this statement was made to the group by none other than Oral Roberts himself:

> *We are also leaders who are recognized as those who believe in and preach the importance of signs and wonders. I personally do not believe that the Gospel can be fully preached without signs and wonders.*

What a bizarre statement!

Whatever happened to Billy Graham and Jimmy Swaggart?

These men are known as two great evangelists who preach the Gospel of Jesus Christ, which is the death, burial and resurrection of our Lord Jesus Christ.

Preaching the Gospel is telling people that Jesus died on the cross for their sins and that He then rose from the dead after three days.

But in the eyes of this charismatic leader, Billy Graham and Jimmy Swaggart must be failures.

Why?

Because they must never fully preach the Gospel since "signs and wonders" in the sense implied by Mr. Roberts do not occur.

Jimmy Swaggart is on record as saying that 99 percent of the "miracles and healings" he has witnessed at crusades of some of his friends' healing outreaches actually never do occur.

Other non-Biblical teaching occurs when Christian leaders instruct the audience to repeat certain words as tongues after them. This is pure cosmic Christianity.

There is not one place in the Bible where the Lord Jesus Christ speaks of anything of the sort.

Nowhere does he say, "Come on, repeat after me these words so that you can speak in tongues, and the more you do it the better tongues you will speak."

And so we see ...

Instead, this comes directly from the occult because it is designed to stir within you the serpent spirit.

It is not something a born-again Christian should ever do.

The true tongues of the Bible occurs when the Holy Spirit comes upon you and He creates the tongues within you.

When you understand the teachings of many charismatic leaders — men who unfortunately command a large audience — you see they really are leading people down the wrong path. I have met many people who have suffered and have been hurt through these teachings of cosmic Christianity. We must alert people to some of the deceptions being thrown at them today.

We want to remember that in the end times those performing signs and wonders will not be the born-again believers but rather Satan's legions. 2 Thessalonians 2: 3, 8-9 says:

Antichrist Associates

"Let no man deceive you by any means because then shall that wicked be revealed, who the Lord shall consume with the spirit of his mouth, and shall destroy with the brightness of his coming, even him, whose coming is after the working of Satan with all power and signs and lying wonders."

False signs, bogus wonders.

The tragedy is that most of the faith healings you see in television ministries today are fake.

These ministers will pronounce healings on individuals who wobble off the stage, while the rest of the audience is going into hysteria.

These are "signs and lying wonders," and we have seen many of these ministers exposed in recent national newscasts.

It is hurting so many people that we need to alert God's children of the dangers and teach them how to maintain discernment.

Having attended some of Oral Roberts' meetings, I failed to see any such signs and wonders take place.

Several ORU graduates who happen to be very good friends of mine also failed to see any in their four-year pursuits of degrees at Oral Roberts University.

Change in theology?

The May-April 1986 issue of *Abundant Life* magazine, published by the Oral Roberts Evangelistic Association gives us some answers as to what Oral Roberts believes about healing and the Word of God.

On page 10 of the magazine, we find the following,

Almost every healing I've ever experienced personally and every healing I've seen in someone else has been a **process** *of healing. Most people don't get sick or defeated or bankrupt or divorced because of what happens in a single day. We get down over a period of time.*

That seems to me to be a far departure of what I've heard from the lips of one who has told people *they were healed* when he laid his hands on them.

I am sure the reruns and films of his crusades would easily reveal a great departure from what he has been telling his followers for many years.

And on page 10, he says:
> The Bible says that 'faith cometh by hearing, and hearing by the word of God' (Romans 10:17) ...
>
> It says faith cometh by hearing. Most of us think about hearing in relationship to other people. 'Did you hear what the preacher said?'
>
> 'Did you hear what he said ... or she said ... about a matter?' But the fact is that you also are **what you yourself say.** [Emphasis ours] And when it comes right down to it, people who have studied the way we learn tell us that we remember only about 10 percent of what other people say to us.
>
> Only about that much lodges in us and becomes a part of our memories. On the other hand, we remember about 90 percent of what we ourselves have to say! Now, what does that mean to you and me today? It means that our own words are even more important to our faith than the words we hear from other people. What you say directly impacts how you believe! [Emphasis ours]

Not necessarily the Word of God

All of the quasi-Christian cults are known by the fact they all claim to speak the Word of God. That is, their words are as important as the words of the Bible because they are speaking "Thus saith the Lord."

This is an extremely important part of all cults. No orthodox Christian church or pastor/teacher would ever make such a claim.

Let no man deceive you.

I would like to share one final "insiders' report" on the reported visions and messages Oral Roberts has said he received from Jesus.

Give Me That Prime-Time Religion, an Insider's Report on the Oral Roberts Evangelistic Association was published by the Oklahoma Book Publishing Company, Inc., and was written by former Oral Roberts staffer Jerry Sholes.

Sholes gives some interesting insights into Oral Roberts' ministry.

He worked for Oral Roberts as a television writer and associate producer. Because of that, he worked very closely with Oral Roberts.

The book is close to 200 pages long, but we will only look at the part which deals with Oral Roberts' "vision" to build the City of Faith.

Antichrist Associates

Sholes says on page 191:
> As difficult as it is to accept ... and I had some problems with this myself ... the City of Faith is **based upon lies.** [emphasis his] The shocking fact is that Oral Roberts, personally, is responsible for those lies ...
>
> Because of personal involvement on my part in the promotion of the City of Faith, and because of my participation in various planning and strategy sessions relating to the City of Faith, I know and am witness to the fact that Oral Roberts has personally lied about the City of Faith. Those lies and the nature of them ... Oral telling millions of people that God told him to do something ... are what made me decide to write this book.

As you can imagine, a great many other people were shocked to hear of such evil in the Kingdom of God.

Just what was Sholes referring to?
> On September 7, 1977, Oral Roberts announced the City of Faith ... In making his announcement, Oral conveyed that he had experienced **a vision in the desert in August 1977,** and that **God had spoken to him and had given him all the**

details for the three-building complex ... [emphasis his] However, in January 1977, Oral Roberts and Ron Smith, Oral's executive vice president, met in my office and discussed with me a three-building complex which would include a clinic, a research center and a hotel ... That discussion took place before Oral's announcement and 7 months before he had his "vision" in the desert. In that conversation, Oral Roberts personally stated that he thought it would cost over $100 million to build the complex ... and that as he improved his personal fund-raising skills, he "needed to find thicker fleece to pick." That's a verbatim quote from a "man of God."

A different set of tales

Oral claimed to have had a vision in the desert and a close associate, Jerry Sholes attests that it was a lie and says that he has the documented proof to that effect.

In light of these statements, we think of the passage in II Peter 2:1-3:

But there were false prophets also among the people, even as there shall be false teachers among you, who priv-

ily shall bring in damnable heresies, even denying the Lord that bought them, and bring upon themselves swift destruction. And many shall follow their pernicious ways; by reason of whom the way of truth shall be evil spoken of. And through covetousness shall they with feigned words make merchandise of you: whose judgment now of a long time lingereth not, and their damnation slumbereth not.

We want to remember that in the end times, the Bible clearly tells us that those performing signs and wonders will not be the people of God.

We read in II Thessalonians 2:3, 8-9:

Let no man deceive you by any means: ... And then shall that Wicked be revealed, whom the Lord shall consume with the spirit of his mouth, and shall destroy with the brightness of his coming: Even him, whose coming is after the working of Satan with all power and signs and lying wonders.

The tragedy is:

Most of the faith healers you see are actually fake healers. Ministers will pronounce healings on individuals who wobble off the stage while the audience goes into hysteria.

These are some of the signs and lying wonders we read about in the Bible that would come.

But the most important action for you or anyone is to establish your relationship with the Lord Jesus Christ.

Make sure you have experienced forgiveness of personal sins through the sacrifice of our Lord Jesus.

Repent of your sins and turn to Him.

11

Evil Devices, Hidden Plans

Central America's biggest troublemaker is the supposedly Marxist, terror-exporting military state of Nicaragua. Look in your encyclopedia for a picture of the Nicaraguan flag. Examine this vicious government's national banner.

In the middle of it for all to see is a pyramid — with rays shooting out of the occultic triangle. Notice, too, the little horn.

Familiar?

Did it get there by chance?

By coincidence?

Hardly!

These are the same symbols you'll find in all of the worldwide, esoteric groups that we've discussed.

This is the official flag of the Republic of Nicaragua.

Antichrist Associates

It's not the flag of the old government — the old Somoza regime that had its faults, but was friendly to the United States.

This is the new flag of the Sandinistas, the so-called Communist revolutionaries now ruling Nicaragua. I don't believe they really are Communists.

They're something far worse.

Communism is anti-God and anti-religious.

The symbols on this new flag are unquestionably religious — but darkly and occultly so.

Recently we've all been watching President Reagan attempt to gain Congressional approval for $100 million in support for Nicaragua's counter-revolutionary forces, the Contras, the "Freedom Fighters."

Now, remembering this symbol of the triangle with radiating sun rays — which, as you recall is on the back of the United States one-dollar bill — consider this irony:

Despite the posturing and grandiose endorsements by bureaucrats in our government, we are secretly, quietly allowing $200 million to go to the Sandinistas.

Twice as much as for the Contras.

Two million dollars are being quietly siphoned to declared enemies of the United States.

Bureaucrats are sending this money through the World Bank, diverting it through European banks, straight into the hands of the Sandinistas.

How can this be?

There are Luciferians well entrenched in the positions of power within the top agencies of our government.

They are outwardly proclaiming support for the Contras.

Yet, haven't you been perplexed at how they make only weak, token appeals for the $100 million President Reagan wants?

Repeatedly Congress has refused to send the money while, strangely, the administration's workers just drag their feet.

Why aren't they aggressively carrying out the President's wishes?

Because they are surreptitiously and clandestinely aiding the enemy — their cohorts in Satan, the occultic Sandinistas.

You see, this is the way Luciferians work.

Antichrist Associates

In secret.
In the dark.
That's what occult means.
Dark.
Shadows.
In secret, they dispatch funding for their diabolical endeavors ... with your and my tax dollars.

That's right.

These people are sending to the enemies of all that is good the hard-earned cash of born-again, Bible-believing Christians. These are dollars dutifully paid in United States federal taxes, wages earned by Americans who love the Lord Jesus Christ, who would do anything — even die — for this country's freedom.

This money is coming from people like you who are dedicated to spreading the Gospel worldwide.

And it's being given to the enemy.

Unchallenged.
Why do I tell you about this?
To discourage you?
So that you will quake in fear at the power of Satan?
No.
Should it discourage you?
No.

It certainly doesn't discourage me.

Instead, it confirms my faith.

That's right!

It strengthens my belief in the Bible. Thousands of years ago, God's Word predicted all of these things would happen.

"... when you see all these things come to pass, look up, because your redemption draweth nigh," counsel the Scriptures.

So, all these apparent victories by Satan's lackeys, are just fulfillments of prophecy — signs to you and me that Jesus' return is coming very, very soon.

I'm excited about that.

I've been enthused for quite a while. And the more the Lord allows me to see of what's taking place today, the more thrilled I become.

No, don't let all these terrible things drag you down.

These fulfillments of prophecy just justify our trust in God.

They show us that we have no other possible hope but our great Father.

The One True One.

Jehovah of the Holy Bible.

God.

There are perhaps two, four or even five billion gods running around this earth — if you would believe the claims of the New Agers.

They'd have us all believe the lie Satan told Eve, that we can all become gods — that we are gods or even God Himself.

Of course, that's a sham, a blasphemous deceit that began in the Garden of Eden.

It's the humanist lie:

That we are the highest being. That we alone set our destinies. That we alone make the rules. And that we, mighty humans, can do anything if we put our great minds to work.

Don't believe it.

It doesn't work.

There is only one God.

He's the Most High God.

There is none like Him and there are none that shall ever be like Him. He is the Creator. He's the Author. And He's the Finisher.

He's written the last page and He knows what is on the bottom line.

Unfortunately, a lot of people refuse to believe in Him.

They prefer believing only in

themselves. Just as they've been taught to do in this country's public schools.

They prefer humanism's glitter. They enjoy believing that they are gods — the wonderful product of some great biological, evolutional, universal throw of the dice.

And God, in His mercy, does not infringe on their free choice — or their ghastly choice of where they will spend eternity.

Whether they will know the truth is up to you and me.

Only you and I can proclaim the truth down here on Earth.

God doesn't send his angels to preach.

Just you and me.

So, our job is before us.

And the eyes of those led astray will be unblinded.

If we are faithful.

But if we are not ...?

The cover story of *Christianity Today*'s May 16, 1986 edition details the New Age religion that is rapidly flooding our society.

The New Agers, too, use the all-seeing eye and triangle as a signal to fellow travelers in the other branches of the occult — just as do to the Mormons in the sunburst window of their Salt Lake City temple.

Just as do the Roman Catholics with the all-seeing eyes in the great stained-glass windows of such beautiful cathedrals as the ones in Munich, Germany, and Frankfort.

So, we are to be wary servants of the Lord — innocent as lambs, but wise as serpents.

Why?

The conspiracy to place demonic symbols everywhere is no re-specter of persons.

You'll find the same all-seeing eye glaring down at you from the beautiful window of the Bethlehem Baptist Temple in Ludlow — which was once the Saint Boniface Catholic Church, before the Baptist congregation bought the building.

Evil symbols.

Proclaiming lies.

Encouraging the slaves of darkness. If you've been a part of any of these movements, don't just be a hearer of the Word as you read this today.

Act on what I'm saying. Separate yourself from these movements. If you're a Christian and a Mason, too, decide which way you are going to go.

Choose the true God.

Leave the darkness behind you.

Immerse yourself in the pureness of God's Word.

Find a Bible-believing church that stands on the truth, that preaches salvation, holiness and God's love — and that is looking for the imminent return of the Lord Jesus Christ.

Beware of groups using these symbols.

Don't look for answers among the Mormons — despite their clever, wholesome television ads now appearing in your and my living rooms on nightly network television.

Theirs is the way of the occult.

Of the ram's head and the inverted five-pointed star.

You've seen this same symbol on Satanist rock singers' albums and on the T-shirts that they sell our unknowing children.

The pentagram.

Witchcraft at its worst.

Antichrist Associates

Attend any occult teaching seminar or psychic fair or witches convention and one of the first things you'll see in the symbols that they so proudly flaunt is this upside-down, hellward-pointing star — and in it the ram's head.

And you'll find it, too, in a place of honor and prominence at the Mormon Temple in Salt Lake City.

The pentagram.

What power does it have?

What harm does it do, say in the rosette window of a Gothic cathedral?

Indeed, what is all the hoopla over symbols?

These evil symbols serve as amulets. Idols.

Cosmic antennas.

In the Old Testament — in Deuteronomy — the Israelites were told such symbols were abominations that they were never to allow them in their homes.

The only thing that could be done with such evil was destruction by sledge hammer and fire.

Amulets.

Fetishes.

Symbols.

Idols.

Talismen to draw the presence of demonic spirits.

Allurements to summon evil, fallen, cursed angels.

Symbols.

Symbols of dark power.

Such as the compass, square and upside-down star of the Freemasons.

Mormon leader Brigham Young wore this cursed talisman on his breast pocket.

So do Hindu "holy men."

So did the evil Egyptian sorcerers who kept the ancient Pharoahs in bondage to Satan's superstition, darkness and death.

The compass represents the male or the heavenly bodies. The square represents the female or the earth. As the rains and the sun's rays fall upon the earth, it becomes fruitful and blossoms and gives birth. You'll notice how the compass is always on top. There are sexual symbols here.

Man and woman.

Intercourse. Mother Earth.

Father Heavens. What about the triangle? It represents the same as the sign of the serpent.

Antichrist Associates

Both are subtle representations of the phallus — the male sexual organ — the blending of the opposites of whatever sort to bring "divine equilibrium."

In Masonic symbology, you see the ominous "G." Just what does it represent?

Ask any Mason.

If a member of the Masonic Lodge sees it on the lapel or ring or license tag or tie tack of a stranger, he knows instantly that he's in the presence of a "brother Mason."

But what does that "G" mean?

Ask any "brother Mason," and he will proudly tell you that it represents the divine Grand Architect of the Universe.

Isn't that nice!

Our Lord, right?

Don't assume that for a moment. Lucifer loves to steal God's glory for himself.

Just who is this grand architect?

Masonic literature will tell you that "It is in the royal arch degree that the secret name of the god of masonry is revealed.

"His name is Jaobulon."

Jaobulon?

Look further and you will find that "Jao" is the Greek word for Jehovah and "bul" is representative of the ancient demon-god Baal — in whose fire thousands of babies were sacrificed alive in Biblical times.

What about "on"?

It is a term used in Babylonian mysteries to call upon the ancient Egyptian God Osiris.

By Masonic tradition, no royal arch mason can pronounce the entire sacred name by himself.

Instead three such Masons will actually entwine their arms together and call upon this secret, blasphemous name of their Grand Architect.

They freely go through this horrible act of blasphemy — many ignorantly allowing themselves to defile the name of the Lord, believing that they are just having a good, fraternal time with lodge brothers.

Instead, they dance with the devil.

Recently, I obtained a copy of the Bible of Freemasonry. It's full of demonic symbols and amulets and evil.

Worse than that, however, it professes to be good.

Antichrist Associates

It pretends to be Biblical.

Many Masons believe that what they do at the Lodge is sufficient to get them into heaven — and that church attendence is unnecessary.

But the deception goes deeper.

It permeates Freemasonry.

In their Bible you'll find a picture that supposedly is a front elevation of King Solomon's Temple, which the Masons claim to have helped build. But look at this "temple!" It's nothing but the evil Tower of Babel, around which sprung Babylon. Remember: the Bible declared that a Babylonian system would — and has — replaced itself — within this symbology of King Solomon's Temple.

And in their Bible you'll see the Eastern Gate of King Solomon's temple.

But, wait!

I've been to Jerusalem.

And this Eastern Gate is bogus!

Instead, it strongly resembles Babylon's Ishtar gate in northern Iraq, just outside of Mosul, a city about 300 miles north of Baghdad. I've been there, too.

I took a train up one evening and got there the next morning.

Why would the writers of this Freemasonry Bible go to such lengths of deception?

Why is this temple — the Tower of Babel, the scene of history's great mutiny against the Lord God — so important to Freemasonry?

Why is the name "Solomon" so important in Freemasonry?

Because it is all more perversion.

Martin Wagoner — who has studied the evil, occultic ways of the Freemasons — says that the Solomon of the Masons is not the Solomon of the Bible. It, instead, is a composite, just like Jaobulon. It comes from "sol" — the Latin word for the sun — from "om," which is a very sacred Hindu monosyllable, and "on" ... again calling on the name of Osiris.

Wagoner says it was designed to show the unity of several god ideas of these various cults.

In other words:

Blasphemy.

Naive Christians are led to believe that King Solomon was a Mason. And, blindly, they are led to worship pagan dieties who are not imaginary, but are real and straight from the pits of hell.

Antichrist Associates

Consider this statement in 1889 from Albert Pike, then the sovereign pontiff of Universal Freemasonry:

To you, sovereign grand inspectors general, we say this, that you may repeat it to the brethren of the 32nd, 31st and 30th degrees:
The masonic religion should be maintained in the purity of the Luciferian doctrine.

Don't miss this:

If Lucifer were not god, would Adonay, the god of the Christians, whose deeds prove as to his cruelty, perfidy and hatred of men, barbarism and revulsion for science, would Adonay and his priests calumniate him?

... Yes, Lucifer is God and, unfortunately, Adonay is also god.

(That is Jesus Christ, the God of the Bible.) The doctrine of satanism is a heresy and the true and pure philosophical religion is the belief in Lucifer, the equal of Adonay.

But Lucifer, the god of good is struggling for humanity against Adonay, the God of darkness and evil."

Indeed, the lines have been drawn.

The battle is raging.
Now, on whose side will you fight?

Note that this esoteric organization clearly stated Lucifer was the good God and that Adonay, Jesus, was the evil god.

The Holy Scriptures tell us in Jude 1:4:

... there are certain men crept in unawares, ... ungodly men, turning the grace of our God into lasciviousness, and denying the only Lord God and our Lord Jesus Christ.

Indeed!
There would be certain men crept in unawares to attempt to destroy the doctrines of the Bible. This is precisely what has taken place in some of the newer translations of the Bible.

For instance, in the *Amplified Bible*, we read in Isaiah 14:12:

How are you fallen from heaven, O light-bringer and day-star, son of the morning! How you are cut down to the ground, you who weakened and laid prostrate the nation [O blasphemous, satanic king of Babylon!]

The King James Version of the

Bible had Lucifer in the place where the Amplified Bible replaced Lucifer with "Light-bringer."

Light bringer?

A footnote at the bottom of the page of the Amplified Bible gives this reason for replacing the name Lucifer with Light-bringer.

"Light-bringer" or "shining one" was originally translated Lucifer, but because of the association of that name with Satan, it is not now used. Some students feel that the application of the name Lucifer to Satan, in spite of the long and confident teaching to that effect is erroneous."

Because some students of the Bible felt that the application of the name Lucifer is erroneous, they changed it to Light-bringer to take away the connotation from Lucifer that he is the blasphemous satanic king of Babylon!

This would seem that some Luciferians have crept in unawares to the translation committee and effectively turned the grace of our God into lasciviousness.

But remember that these people want to picture Lucifer as the good God and Jesus as the evil god. The

New International Version may give that impression to some who may read this passage.

Isaiah 14: 12 in the NIV reads like this, "How you have fallen from heaven, O morning star, son of the dawn! You have been cast down to the earth, you who once laid low the nations!"

En evil deception

When I first read that passage in the NIV, the first thing my mind thought of was Jesus Christ.

In that understanding, these people accomplished their mission, if that mission was to make Jesus appear as the evil god.

II Corinthians 11:13-14 becomes more important to Bible students as things such as this continue to pervert the things of God.

We read "For such are false apostles, deceitful workers, transforming themselves into the apostles of Christ.

"And no marvel: for Satan himself is transformed into an angel of light."

Questions for Robert Schuller

In the Opinion section of the May 1983 issue of *Moody* magazine, Dr. John MacArthur reviewed the book,

Antichrist Associates

Self-Esteem — The New Reformation. Dr. MacArthur had a personal conversation with Dr. Schuller about this review since Dr. Schuller was the author.

Dr. MacArthur says the book is "quasi-Christian, positive humanism."

He then noted:

Martin Marty, whom Schuller quotes in the opening, was right in suggesting,

"Is not this a philosophy which makes room for God more than a theology that incorporates psychology?"

The article goes on to say,

Schuller has said, "To be born again means that we must be changed from a negative to a positive self-image (p. 68).

God says, "You purify your soul in obeying the truth, being born again by the Word of God" (I Peter 1:22, 23).

This statement by Dr. Schuller on how to be born again is of the utmost importance because it pertains to a person's eternal destiny.

Dr. Schuller is not using the Bible literally in the true sense that has been supported by historical Christianity by Dr. Schuller. In another crucial part of our redemption story, we quote this from the *Moody* magazine article,

When Schuller says, 'The cross protected our Lord's perfect self-esteem from turning into sinful pride' (p. 75), what psychological implications is he relating to the Son of God and what is he saying about Christ's impeccability (p. 75)? Why does Schuller rank Jesus with Freud, Adler and Frankl, as if He were a psychiatrist (pg 79), then Scripture affirms His utter pre-eminence (Col. 1: 15-19)? Schuller says, 'The most serious sin is the one that causes me to say, I am unworthy ...

For once a person believes he is an unworthy sinner, it is doubtful if he can really honestly accept the saving grace God offers in Jesus Christ (p. 98). Is not this opposite the message of the Lord Jesus which confronts a person's sin and calls him to repent and be converted (Matt. 4:17)?

Dr. John MacArthur sums up Dr. Schuller's book review with these comments, "Neo-orthodoxy, existentialism, liberalism and humanism weave their way through the book and reveal Schuller's lack of total commitment to an authoritative Scripture which is able to perfect the believer. Schuller's book falls into this formula of converting nobody."

In conclusion:

In conclusion, our hearts' desire is that each reader will make it his duty to try the spirits to see if they are of God. We pray that if you were involved in any of these esoteric groups and/or quasi-Christian organizations, that you will investigate for yourself the writings and claims of such signs and wonders and put them to the test.

We are not hoping to change the entire system and bring them under the Lordship of Christ Jesus.

Yet, on the other hand ...

We know this is not what the Bible says will happen. But on the contrary, we read in II Timothy 3:13-17,

But evil men and seducers shall wax worse, deceiving, and being deceived. But continue thou in the things which thou hast learned and hast been assured of, knowing of

whom thou hast learned them; ... that from a child thou hast known the holy scriptures, which are able to make thee wise unto salvation through faith which is in Christ Jesus.

Trust the Lord

We leave you with those precious words and trust if you have not experienced the forgiveness sins that you will place your trust in the Lord Jesus Christ.

He died and paid the penalty for all your sins and rose gloriously from the dead and stands alive today offering to you the gift of eternal life.

The Bible says all have sinned and come short of the glory of God.

You cannot save yourself

You must be born again.
Ask Jesus to forgive you.
If you ask Him, He will!

Yes, send me the following books and/or tapes:

_______ copy (copies) of Antichrist Associates and Cosmic Christianity @ $5.95   = $ _______
_______ copy (copies) of America Betrayed! @ $5.95   = $ _______
_______ copy (copies) of A Planned Deception @ $8.95   = $ _______
_______ copy (copies) of A Reasonable Reason to Wait @ $4.95   = $ _______
_______ copy (copies) of Backward Masking Unmasked @ $5.95   = $ _______
_______ copy (copies) of Backward Masking Unmasked Cassette Tape @ $6.95   = $ _______
_______ copy (copies) of Devil Take the Youngest @ $6.95   = $ _______
_______ copy (copies) of Edmund Burke and the Natural Law @ $7.95   = $ _______
_______ copy (copies) of Globalism: America's Demise @ $6.95   = $ _______
_______ copy (copies) of Gates of Brass (The Voice of Russian Jews Denied Visas to Israel) @ $5.95   = $ _______
_______ copy (copies) of Honor Thy Father/ Exposing the Secret World of Incest @ $5.95   = $ _______
_______ copy (copies) of More Rock, Country & Backward Masking Unmasked @ $5.95   = $ _______
_______ copy (copies) of More Rock, Country & Backward Masking Unmasked Tape @ $6.95   = $ _______
_______ copy (copies) of Rest From the Quest @ $5.95   = $ _______
_______ copy (copies) of The Cult Explosion @ $6.95   = $ _______
_______ copy (copies) of The God Makers @ $6.95   = $ _______
_______ copy (copies) of The Great Debate of Creation Versus Evolution @ $4.95   = $ _______
_______ copy (copies) of The Hidden Dangers of the Rainbow @ $6.95   = $ _______
_______ copy (copies) of The Hidden Dangers of the Rainbow Seminar Tapes @ $19.95   = $ _______
_______ copy (copies) of The Seduction of Christianity @ $7.95   = $ _______
_______ copy (copies) of The Twisted Cross @ $7.95   = $ _______
_______ copy (copies) of Who Will Rise Up? @ $5.95   = $ _______
_______ copy (copies) of Antichrist Associates and Cosmic Christianity — 5-program Video @ $100   = $ _______
_______ copy (copies) of Antichrist Associates and Cosmic Christianity — Audio Casettes @ $25   = $ _______
_______ copy (copies) of Alexander Scourby/King James Bible Audio Casette @ $150   = $ _______
_______ copy (copies) of Alexander Scourby/King James Bible Audio Casette — New Testament @ $50   = $ _______
_______ copy (copies) of Gates of Brass video @ $75   = $ _______

Childrens Books and Tapes
State of The Heart Series

_______ copy (copies) of Happy Feet @ $10   = $ _______
_______ copy (copies) of More Than A Friend @ $10   = $ _______
_______ copy (copies) of Use It Or Lose It @ $10   = $ _______
_______ copy (copies) of You Can Be A Winner @ $10   = $ _______
_______ copy (copies) of You Don't Know My Dad @ $10   = $ _______

Stories That Live Series

_______ copy (copies) of Adam and Eve @ $10   = $ _______
_______ copy (copies) of Daniel and The Lions @ $10   = $ _______
_______ copy (copies) of David and Goliath @ $10   = $ _______
_______ copy (copies) of God Is Good @ $10   = $ _______
_______ copy (copies) of Jesus Is Alive @ $10   = $ _______
_______ copy (copies) of Jesus Loves Me @ $10   = $ _______
_______ copy (copies) of Joseph: The Dreamer @ $10   = $ _______
_______ copy (copies) of Man of Miracles @ $10   = $ _______
_______ copy (copies) of Special Friends @ $10   = $ _______
_______ copy (copies) of Stories of Jesus @ $10   = $ _______
_______ complete set of 10 "Stories That Live" @ $75   = $ _______

Order direct from Today, The Bible and You, P.O. Box 1722, Broken Arrow, OK 74013.

Send check/money order or for faster service VISA/Mastercard orders call toll-free (In Oklahoma) 1-800-722-5660. All other states call 1-800-232-1616.

Enclosed is $__________

Name ____

Address ____

City __________________________________ State ______ Zip__________

ISBN: 0-9617286-0-4